The 20 British Prime Ministers
of the 20th century

Eden

PETER WILBY

HAUS PUBLISHING · LONDON

First published in Great Britain in 2006 by
Haus Publishing Limited
26 Cadogan Court
Draycott Avenue
London SW3 3BX

www.hauspublishing.co.uk

A CIP catalogue record for this book is available from the British Library

ISBN 1-904950-65-5

Designed by BrillDesign
Typeset in Garamond 3 by MacGuru Ltd
info@macguru.org.uk

Printed and bound by Graphicom, Vicenza

Front cover: John Holder

Contents

Part One

THE LIFE

Chapter 1: Early Life and Career: 1897–1931

Robert Anthony Eden was born into the lower rungs of the English aristocracy at Windlestone Hall, near Bishop Auckland, on 12 June 1897. His father's baronetcy went back to 1672 and the family's ownership of property in the area to the 15th century. His family were, in every respect, members of the ruling class and it was natural that Eden should, at some stage, consider a career in public life. On his father's side, his ancestors included, as well as numerous MPs, a mistress of Charles II, a former governor of Maryland and, more improbably, the author of an 18th-century study of the poor which Karl Marx was later to praise. On his mother's side, his forebears included Lord Grey, who piloted the Great Reform Bill through Parliament in 1832.

Eden's childhood world comprised ponies, governesses, garden parties, a flat (later a house) in London as well as an estate in Durham, hunting, shooting, servants and, among the adults, incipient gout. Yet his immediate family was far from conventional. His irascible, spendthrift father, Sir William Eden, was prone to uncontrollable rages, during which he was reported to have bitten a carpet, to have ejected an unwanted joint of lamb from the window, and to have beheaded instantly any red flowers in the garden. The last was for aesthetic rather than political reasons. Sir William was an art collector and water-colourist, as well as a keen amateur boxer. The family social circle included the champion boxer 'Bombardier' Billy Wells as well as the novelist George Moore, the artist Walter Sickert and the critic Max Beerbohm.

Eden's mother, though more attentive to her children than her husband, had something of Dickens' Mrs Jellyby about her. She was absorbed in charitable work – for example, raising money to build a miners' cottage hospital in Bishop Auckland – to such an extent that Eden observed: *I think my mother preferred the simpler relationship ... between donor and recipient to the more complicated one between mother and child.*[1] As if Eden's childhood were not already strange enough, it was punctuated by visits to the estate from an inmate of the local lunatic asylum, who believed she was herself Lady Eden and, therefore, the children's mother. It was probably not until he was an adult, however, that he heard the rumours, almost certainly false, that his real father was not Sir William but a handsome, dashing Conservative MP who may have struck up an extra-marital liaison with his mother.

Against this background, Eden grew into an introverted, serious, bookish child. Even when he played soldiers with his three brothers, his father noted, he carried a book under his arm. Of his Durham home, Eden wrote: *I loved its spaciousness and the knowledge that within it I could find beauty, reading and entertainment for any mood ... my father had created Windlestone, as only an artist could, as a personal harmony.*[2]

Eden attended prep schools in Kensington and Surrey and then went on to Eton, where he was a strong oarsman, as well as being outstanding at languages and absorbed by art and literature. But he was never a star at school and he was far from happy.

All the same, it was a sheltered, privileged life. Like almost every member of the ruling class in Edwardian England, Eden expected it to go on for ever. Britain had not fought a major Continental war for nearly a century; the Labour Party was still in its infancy with fewer than 50 MPs; and the Russian Revolution had yet to take place. *It all seemed so permanent,* wrote Eden, ... *Why should it end in any of our lifetimes?*[3] Even as the First World War approached, one of his Eton masters, echoing the common view, said: 'There won't be any war, the City would never allow it.' If there were fighting, it would last only months, if not weeks.

It all seemed so permanent, ...Why should it end in any of our lifetimes?

EDEN

Like many young men of his generation, Eden was keen to serve in the war and volunteered in September 1915 (conscription was not introduced until 1916) while still at school. Since he suffered from short-sighted astigmatism, Eden was by no means certain he would be accepted. But through the Earl of Feversham, a close family friend known as 'Charlie' and a relative by marriage, he was commissioned as a second lieutenant in a yeomanry regiment, recruited largely from farmers' sons and estate workers in the north-east. After training, he and his regiment reached the Continent in April 1916. Their chief fear was that the war might be over before they got there.

To an 18-year-old of Eden's background, the reality must have been devastating. Years later, he recalled *the stench, the mud, the corpses, the destruction everywhere, the torn and twisted guns and limbers, the shattered wagons, the mutilated horses and mules* and, at a casualty clearing station, *the crowded tents ... the tired surgeons, the bandaged figures, most of them silent on their stretchers and still in their torn and muddied uniforms.*[4] His mother sent expensive chocolates to Flanders, which Eden decided to keep for Christmas. After a single night in the trenches, rats – *more like buck rabbits in size*, recalled Eden – had nibbled every one.

It is hard now to grasp the enormity of what happened to Eden's generation. In the Battle of the Somme alone, nearly 100,000 British and Empire troops were killed, including nearly 20,000 on the first day. The death toll among junior officers was roughly 50 per cent higher than among the ranks. At least a third of Eden's contemporaries at Eton were lost. Nor did the conflict spare Eden's family. His eldest brother Jack was killed in the first months. The next brother, Tim, was in Germany when war broke out and therefore interned. A little later, Sir William died, albeit of natural causes. Eden himself had to recover Charlie Feversham's body by night in no man's land and bury it at dawn under enemy fire. But the greatest blow was the loss of his younger brother Nicholas, drowned at just 16 when his ship went down in the Battle of Jutland. Nicholas was his closest childhood friend. *For as long as I could remember*, wrote Eden, *we had shared everything, nannies, governesses, tutors, ponies ... we preferred each other's company to any other in the world.*[5]

The regiment Eden joined in 1915 was the 21st Battalion the Yeoman Rifles, of the King's Royal Rifle Corps. The Secretary of State for War, Lord Kitchener, had organised numerous regiments of this type for his 'New Armies', raised entirely by voluntary enlistment. The yeomanry regiments had a strong local identity, and to encourage enlistment men were told that they and their friends would all serve together. But when such units suffered heavy casualties, all too frequently on the Western Front, the impact at home was increased by communities losing most of a generation of young men at the same time.

To Eden, therefore, *death in battle seemed, if not normal, at least acceptable.*[6] It was shortly after learning of Nicholas' death that, leading a night-time mission to the German trenches, he came under enemy fire. His sergeant was wounded and Eden stayed, applying a tourniquet to staunch the bleeding, until a stretcher came. He then helped carry him back to the British lines in full view of the enemy. For this, he was awarded the Military Cross, though it is not mentioned in his memoirs or in any letter home that survives.

Eden, who fought in major battles at the Somme and Ypres, had what people call a good war. He became, as a result of the high casualty rate, one of the youngest adjutants in the Army and, by the end of it, he was a brigade major. He had by then left his yeomanry regiment, which had been specially formed to attract volunteers with the promise that they could fight alongside men of similar social and regional background. *We had enlisted together, trained together, fought together*, he wrote. This experience, he insisted later, taught him the *irrelevance and unreality of class distinction*.[7]

If Eden omits to mention his MC in his memoirs, he also omits to explain how and why he went into politics. He gives the impression he drifted into Parliament almost by accident rather as a young man of a later generation might drift off to Uganda on voluntary service. In fact, even at school, he wasn't exactly apolitical. He exulted in Conservative election victories, and despised Winston Churchill, then a Liberal. During the war, he developed, like most serving soldiers, a vigorous dislike of politicians, whom he described to his mother as *unscrupulous ... narrow-minded, self-satisfied, crassly ignorant* and to his sister as *brutes and murderers*.[8]

That didn't stop him fixing his sights on a political career. Since one elder brother had survived the war, he wasn't going to inherit the family estate and therefore needed work. His eyesight would be a handicap in an army career and he didn't like the idea of university because, he wrote to his mother, he had been *ordering other people about and holding a position of great responsibility* for three years.[9] So, he wrote to his brother, *I am thinking very seriously of standing for Parliament*.[10] He had asked *dear Mama* to inquire about Bishop Auckland as a possible seat, where his father had chaired the Conservative Association. Though nothing came of that, his thoughts of other careers were influenced by political ambition. He thought the Colonial Service in Africa might be an advantage *if I go in for politics*. His ultimate aim, he told his sister, was *Secretary for Foreign Affairs or something like that*.[11]

In the end, his mother persuaded him to go to Christ Church, Oxford, as his father, elder brother and several ancestors had done. He regarded university politics as beneath him, however. *It all seems such a waste of time and energy*, he told his brother.[12] He never attended Union debates and devoted his time to art and university drama. He founded the Uffizi Society to study painters and his lecture to the society on Cezanne caused, according to a future director of the Tate Gallery, 'something of a sensation'. This man and others noted Eden's 'fine presence' but he made no great impact at university, being, one suspects, too serious, shy and conventional.

While taking his Oxford finals, Eden won the Conservative candidacy for the Durham mining constituency of Spennymoor, thanks largely to his family's neighbour Lord Londonderry, the greatest of the Durham mineowners. He was comfortably defeated in the 1922 general election, not least because he served briefly in the Durham Defence Force when a miners' strike threatened to turn into a general strike the previous year.

Eden, like everybody else of his class at this time, dreaded Labour's seemingly remorseless advance. Mass confiscations of property and savings, an alliance with Bolshevik Russia and even the abolition of marriage were widely feared. Yet Eden never took the diehard Tory view and was already established as a left-wing, 'one nation' Conservative who, for example, advocated better pensions and abolition of the means test for benefits.

Family connections again helped when Eden set his sights – ambitiously, in view of his stilted writing style – on a career as a newspaper contributor. The chairman of the *Yorkshire Post* was Sir Gervase Beckett who had married Feversham's widow and, in that paper, Eden's articles found a home. More important, Beatrice, Beckett's teenage daughter by his first marriage, became the object of Eden's amorous attentions. His attempts to ensnare the classier women at Oxford had failed – perhaps they found him too earnest or too short of money and prospects – and he ended up having a faintly scandalous affair with an actress. Beatrice was on the rebound from a failed romance and Eden, several years older, was exactly the sort of man a father thinks suitable for his daughter. Beckett was a banker, who generously subsidised Eden in his early career, and it was a classic English match between commerce and social status. There was affection, even passion, but more on Eden's side than Beatrice's, and they had little in common. They were married in 1923 at St Margaret's Church in Westminster on the same day that Andrew Bonar Law, the former Prime Minister, was buried a few yards away in the south nave of the Abbey.

By now, the Conservative leader Stanley Baldwin was Prime Minister and Eden had been adopted as a by-election candidate for the safe seat of Warwick and Leamington. The by-election never took place because Baldwin called a surprise general election. Eden won the seat comfortably, against the improbable Labour candidacy of the Countess of Warwick, a mistress of Edward VII and another of his relatives by marriage. But the Conservatives, though returned as the largest single party, failed to get an overall majority. In the New Year of 1924, the Liberals joined Labour in a vote of no confidence in Baldwin and the first Labour government took office. Many, including Eden, had thought it inevitable. Few had expected it so soon; but members of Eden's class were delighted that, with the opposition parties holding more than twice as many Commons seats as the government, Labour could now experience responsibility without the power to do anything that could disturb the established order.

The government fell within the year, brought down by a confidence motion on the Attorney-General's failure to prosecute the editor of a Communist newspaper which had urged soldiers never to fight their fellow workers. By then, Eden had made his maiden Commons speech, insisting on the need for defence against air attack, *the greatest peril of modern war*.

In the October 1924 general election, the Conservatives were returned with a huge majority and the Liberals, who had won 400 seats as recently as 1906, were reduced to a rump of 40. Though it won fewer seats than in the previous election, Labour's share of the vote was up. In the sense that the Conservatives and Labour were now the dominant parties, this was the first Parliament of the modern era.

Eden was a young man in a hurry who feared, when no government position immediately came his way, that *this is going to prove a pretty deadly Parliament*.[13] But Baldwin was already adopting him as his protégé and, in February, Eden got his first break, as a parliamentary private secretary (PPS) at the Home Office. This unpaid and unchallenging position was the first rung on the ministerial ladder. Equally important, from Eden's point of view, it allowed him to continue speaking freely on foreign affairs, as he did often in the Commons, as well as writing a rather dull book, *Places in the Sun*, about his travels abroad. It had a foreword by Baldwin, and sold as badly as it deserved.

It was a measure of Eden's growing reputation that the government briefed him to make a supportive contribution when Austen Chamberlain, the Foreign Secretary and a former party leader, faced a censure motion over his handling of Germany's entry to the League of Nations. A new position, as Chamberlain's PPS, followed in July 1926. This period at the Foreign Office, lasting nearly three years, was an ideal apprenticeship for a future Foreign Secretary. Eden met leading European statesmen, defended an Anglo-French naval agreement in the Commons (close Anglo-French relations were to be one of the bedrocks of Eden's own policies) and attended the League of Nations council in Geneva. By 1928, Clementine Churchill was urging the promotion of 'that nice Captain Eden' in a letter to her husband Winston, then the Chancellor of the Exchequer.[14]

But the shadows that were to haunt Eden nearly all his political life were gathering. His rapid ascent was making enemies; his finances were stretched; his widowed mother, always a spendthrift, was running up debts and apparently creaming off money from the charities she was supposed to raise money for; he had a grumbling appendix and a duodenal ulcer; and, despite the birth of three sons (one of whom died in infancy), he had begun extra-marital affairs, as had his wife. Eden clearly thought the last was potentially the greatest threat to his career, and, in his diary, wrote about his mistresses in Arabic. In reality, the danger was small because the press was then discreet about ruling-class foibles.

The greatest blow was the result of the 1929 general election. Eden expected promotion in the new Parliament. Instead, he found himself in opposition, worrying whether the Conservatives would ever get back. Labour, though still without an overall majority, was for the first time the largest party, and again took office under its leader Ramsay MacDonald.

Eden joined what he called a *loose fraternity* of Tory MPs, and others tartly called 'the YMCA'. *We held the same views*, Eden later wrote, *our domestic politics being to the left of centre in our own party*. One of the group's leading lights, Noel Skelton, had earlier coined the phrase 'property-owning democracy' which Eden and later Harold Macmillan were to make such a feature of their election campaigns in the 1950s. Eden himself, in a speech in 1929, advocated co-partnership in industry and said *the Conservative objective ... must be ... to enable every worker to become a capitalist.*[15]

By this time, Eden was enough of a political figure to be the occasional recipient of MacDonald's confidences which created the impression *that, not only do all the cares of the world rest upon his head, but that nobody can ever have been Prime Minister of England before.*[16] Eden's loyalty to his own party leader was total. By 1930, Baldwin's overthrow seemed inevitable, with the Tory right, supported by the *Daily Express* and *Daily Mail*, in a fury over his resistance to Empire free trade (which would have meant high tariffs against goods from countries outside the Empire) and over his support for self-government in India. *If the Conservative party jettisons Mr Baldwin*, Eden wrote to *The Times*, *it will sacrifice its greatest electoral asset*. He was the barrier to the party becoming *the creature of millionaire newspaper owners or a mere appendage of big business.*[17] Baldwin, helped by good by-election results, survived, and Eden's career duly prospered. His first reward was to become a delegate on an all-party committee on disarmament, which

The Conservative objective ... must be ... to enable every worker to become a capitalist.

EDEN

also included MacDonald, Chamberlain and Lloyd George.

Eden ended his career as a backbencher as he had begun it – with a speech on the need for stronger air defences. Throughout Europe, he warned in June 1931, *the youngest generation is being ... encouraged in military methods of thought and military drill.* He had seen the effects of aerial bombardment in the 1914–18 war. In future, *the safest place will be the front line, if there is one, and the most dangerous the houses of the civilian population.*[18]

Two months later, Britain was plunged into its gravest political crisis of the century. Facing a run on the pound, the Labour Cabinet split over the need for spending cuts. MacDonald tendered his government's resignation, but then immediately returned to office, with a few other leading Labour ministers, as head of a National Government, which also included Liberals but was dominated by Conservatives. Though MacDonald coveted Eden's long-awaited position of Foreign Office under-secretary for his son Malcolm, Baldwin persuaded him to relent. Eden's ministerial career had begun.

Chapter 2: 'The Blue-Eyed Boy': 1931–5

For a brief period, Eden was the only Foreign Office minister in the Commons, since the Secretary of State was Lord Reading. But after an October general election – which the National Government under MacDonald won by the biggest landslide in British history – Reading stood down and Sir John Simon took over.

This appointment was dictated by politics, since the National Government, though overwhelmingly Conservative, had to find senior positions for Labour members of the coalition and for Liberals of whom Simon was one. Between him and Eden, it was not a happy marriage. 'Soapy' Simon, oleaginous, lawyerly and intellectually arrogant, whose smile was compared to a brass plate on a coffin, was almost universally unpopular. Eden thought not only that he was lazy, but also that he was a bad delegator. *He did not want to do the work*, recalled Eden, *yet he could hardly bear anyone else to do it*. Worse, *his brilliant, analytical mind hated to take decisions*.[1]

Yet Simon seems to have held Eden in high regard. So did MacDonald, but Eden saw him, too, as indecisive: *his late Cabinet did not call him MacShuffle for nothing*.[2] Nor was Eden enamoured of the FO's permanent under-secretary, the patrician, condescending and very rich Sir Robert Vansittart, who *was seldom an official giving cool and disinterested advice*, but rather *a fanatical crusader and much more a Secretary of State in mentality than a permanent official*.[3] Here the dislike was mutual: Vansittart came to regard Eden as not only 'second rate but also a dirty dog'.[4]

Eden became, in effect, the minister for disarmament and League of Nations affairs. Most ministers tend to work up enthusiasm for their own brief, because it is the best way of getting noticed. Eden, in his first post, was no exception. Insofar as he was more enthusiastic for disarmament (or, more accurately, arms limitation) than most of his ministerial colleagues, he was the first of the appeasers.

Almost as soon as the National Government took office, the world saw the first act of aggression from what later became the Axis powers: in September 1931, the Japanese occupied large parts of Manchuria, where they, the Russians and the Chinese had long jostled for control. Even diplomatic and military sanctions were too much for British ministers to contemplate. They might lead to war and Britain, which had colonies and trading interests in the Far East, would be in the front line. Eden was then too junior a minister to have any significant impact on Far Eastern policy, but there is no record that he dissented from it, even privately. As pressure grew for League of Nations action, he wrote in a Foreign Office minute that *we with vital interests at stake must ... moderate the zeal of those who have none*.[5]

> '*With France and Spain menaced by Bolshevism ... it might pay us to throw in our lot with Germany and Italy.*'
>
> MAURICE HANKEY

It was not clear then that Japan was a greater threat than emerging Chinese nationalism. Nor was it clear where the threats to European peace would come from. Hitler had still to achieve power. British opinion worried as much about French intransigence in sticking to the harsh terms imposed by the victors at Versailles – which included, for example, depriving Germany of control even of her own rivers, such as the Rhine and the Danube – as about the dangers of a resurgent Germany. As almost every statesman saw it at the time, Versailles was obsolete. A new European settlement was needed.

Mussolini, meanwhile, was widely admired for his anti-Communism and his success in making the trains run on time. Many who feared Germany thought the best answer was to bind Italy into alliance with Britain and France. Others were keener on reaching an understanding with Russia. Others again thought an accommodation with Germany was the best hope of resisting the Bolshevik threat and the best long-term protection for the Empire. Later, after Hitler had come to power, Maurice Hankey, the Cabinet Secretary, would write: 'With France and Spain menaced by Bolshevism ... it might pay us to throw in our lot with Germany and Italy.'[6] Few would take Austen Chamberlain's view, expressed in April 1933, that a country in which 'it is a crime to be in favour of peace and a crime to be a Jew' was not one 'to which we can afford to make concessions'.[7]

Against this background, the world disarmament conference – widely regarded as the most important international conference since Versailles – began in Geneva in February 1932, with Eden taking up almost permanent residence there. The conference made his name. 'He is now the blue-eyed boy,' wrote a Tory MP in his diary, '... a charming young man and an excellent speaker.' One Cabinet member wrote to Baldwin from Geneva: 'Somehow or another Anthony has got the confidence – nay the adulation – of all these strange animals that live in this zoo.'[8] When MacDonald and Simon were due in Geneva to take over at a crucial stage, the British delegation insisted that Eden should stay because, as Eden himself recalled, *I alone understood the problem.*[9]

Yet all Eden's hard work, charm and snappy dressing – an American newspaper poll named him the fourth best-dressed man in Europe and his trademark black Homburg became known as 'the Eden hat' – came to very little. At one stage, Eden drew up a detailed draft disarmament convention – which, among other things, would have banned all bombing aircraft – and got Cabinet backing for it. However, the stumbling block was that, if Germany was to subscribe to an agreement, she had to be allowed something resembling parity with other nations. This meant increasing German armaments while other nations decreased theirs. To this the French, who were most directly vulnerable to a German attack, would not agree, unless Britain gave cast-iron guarantees to come to their aid. On this, Eden's scheme foundered.

The Geneva conference reached a crisis in October 1933, nine months after Hitler came to power. Simon announced Britain could not agree to a convention that provided for immediate German rearmament. The Germans withdrew from the conference and said they would also leave the League of Nations. In his diary, Eden blamed Simon for not driving disarmament forward more vigorously when Hitler's predecessors were in power. *We missed the bus then, and could never overtake it*. In his memoirs, in a rare admission of error, Eden called this *a sweeping and youthful judgment*, acknowledging that Germany had started research on rockets as early as 1930 and that, by autumn 1933, *Hitler was starting to build military aircraft in quantity*.[10]

All the same, ministers were not yet ready to give up on disarmament. None of them – and certainly not Eden – heeded Vansittart's warning that 'the present regime in Germany will … loose off another European war just as soon as it feels strong enough'.[11] Vansittart predicted German annexation of Austria and seizure of Polish land. He advocated economic sanctions against Hitler and even an immediate preventive war. But Vansittart's warnings started before Hitler came to power; his views on Germans bordered on the racist and he was not averse to compromise with Japanese or Italian aggression. Besides, by-election results had ministers in a panic. The Conservatives lost East Fulham to a pro-disarmament Labour candidate on a 26.5 per cent swing. Several other seats were lost on only slightly less dramatic swings.

So 'Mister Disarmament', far from being out of a job, was promoted to Lord Privy Seal, with his duties unchanged. Eden was miffed that he still didn't get a Cabinet seat. But in the New Year of 1934, he set off by train for Paris, Berlin and Rome, to *a grand, if distinctly embarrassing send-off* from the French, German and Italian ambassadors, as well as Simon.[12] His job was to canvass support for a British proposal that Germany rearm over seven years while others disarmed over ten.

This journey – punctuated by fog in the Channel, a collision with the pier at Calais and riots over a financial scandal in France – led to Eden's first meeting with Hitler. *He was restrained and friendly*, wrote Eden in his memoirs, ... *he listened to what I had to say... There were neither fidgets nor exclamations... Hitler impressed me... as much more than a demagogue. He... showed himself completely master of his subject.*[13] If this verdict seems embarrassing, what Eden wrote privately at the time seems even more so. *The new Germany of Hitler and Goebels [sic] is to be preferred to the old*, he wrote to Simon. The *poor man* had been *badly gassed by us* in the 1914–18 war, he wrote to Baldwin, and Eden found it *very hard to believe* he wanted war.[14] *I rather liked him*, he wrote to his wife.[15] Eden

Hitler impressed me... as much more than a demagogue. He... showed himself completely master of his subject.

EDEN

was less effusive about Louis Barthou, the French foreign minister, a long-standing hawk on the enforcement of the Versailles terms and a man who might be described as the first of the anti-appeasers. *Bristly and foxy*, was Eden's verdict, *... a nasty old man at heart.*[16]

His colleagues in London were not at all happy with Eden and his new best friend. True, Hitler had agreed to restrictions on the expansion of the paramilitary SS and SA (which, to the hilarity of the British ambassador, the *Führer* had argued were no different from the Salvation Army or the training corps at Eton) and had conceded that French disarmament need not begin immediately. But Simon and other ministers rebuked Eden for being too accommodating while Vansittart described Hitler's whole package as 'an attractively-baited trap'. The French said no German promises were any good unless there were clear sanctions if Hitler broke them. Of them, Eden used language he would later use of the Germans and Italians. If France were given concessions, *she will ask for more.*[17]

Eden's retrospective justification for his policies was that, if Hitler had broken an agreement so favourable to him, *it would have flashed a clearer warning than breaches of unequal restrictions imposed by the* [First World War] *victors*. Britain and France, he argued, *lost an opportunity to circumscribe Hitler by an agreement which would have deprived his later actions of some spurious pretext, and reinforced allied authority and justification in resisting them.*[18] The Geneva conference held what was in effect its last session in May 1934. But the rise and rise of Anthony Eden continued. In the summer, he was made a Privy Councillor. His reputation was further enhanced that year by two episodes.

First, a plebiscite in the Saar was due in January. This area on the Franco-German border had been governed by an international commission since the First World War. Now, the inhabitants had to decide which country they wished to join and Nazi intimidation was widely feared. Eden wanted to send British troops as part of an international police force. Several ministers, including Simon and Neville Chamberlain, argued that the British didn't want their troops on the Continent again. With Baldwin's backing, Eden got his way. Though the voting gave Germany an overwhelming majority, the policing operation kept the peace.

The second episode seemed more threatening at the time. In October 1934, Louis Barthou and King Alexander of Yugoslavia were assassinated in Marseilles by Croatian terrorists. Both Italy and Hungary were suspected of involvement and Eden saw a parallel with Sarajevo, where an assassination had led to the First World War. Averting a new war, starting in the Balkans and probably spreading, was *my most important and toughest assignment to date*.[19] Eden succeeded.

Pierre Laval (1883–1945) later went on to be a leading figure in the collaborationist Vichy regime after the fall of France in 1940. Having called the meeting of the National Assembly which appointed Pétain president, he served as his deputy from June to December 1940, and he was premier from April 1942, earning popular hatred for supplying French forced labourers for German industries. He escaped to Spain at the end of the war, but was returned to France, where he was tried for treason. He was found guilty and executed by firing squad on 15 October 1945.

He brokered a deal at the League that avoided implicating Italy (though she was almost certainly up to her neck in it) and merely required the Hungarian government to conduct an inquiry. When the Hungarian foreign minister told Pierre Laval, his new French counterpart, that he found the whole formula incomprehensible, Laval replied: 'Excellent!'

With hindsight, a whiff of appeasement can be detected in Eden's handling of both these episodes, but it didn't seem like that at the time. The military adviser to Britain's Geneva delegation, later wrote that 'too much praise cannot be given to Mr Eden' whose 'reputation had spread all over Europe'.[20] As Eden himself put it: *By the end of... 1934, our authority and the League's stood higher than at any time in the National government's life.*[21]

Though disarmament was dead, this was indeed the League's high-water mark. The British public wanted a strong line against the dictators, but they didn't want war and, if they wanted rearmament, they didn't want to pay for it. The League was the way to square this circle. Collective security would keep the peace, people thought. But the League had no more divisions than the Pope: its strength and determination depended on its members. If the League acted, Britain, then easily the strongest European power, would bear the brunt of any fighting that followed. The government's policy throughout 1935 was summed up by a Cabinet minute during the Abyssinian crisis: 'to see the emergency did not develop to the point where the question of fulfilment [of British obligations under the League covenant] arose'.[22]

In March, Eden and Simon again visited Berlin despite announcements that, in defiance of the Versailles terms, Germany now had an air force and proposed to introduce compulsory military service. Eden found Hitler *definitely ... less anxious to please than a year before.*[23] *The old Prussian spirit very much in evidence*, he wrote in his diary.[24] He told his colleagues that it was now *exceedingly difficult* to see a basis for a general European settlement. The way forward was for *the great powers of the League* to reaffirm *their intention to collaborate more closely than ever.*[25] However Simon, who thought Hitler resembled Joan of Arc with a moustache, liked the idea of allowing him to expand eastwards. *I am strongly against it*, Eden recorded.[26] Here were the beginnings of one issue that was to divide British politicians for the rest of the decade.

Eden, without Simon, went on to Moscow, where he was the first Western minister to visit since the 1917 Revolu-.tion. He found *the weather, the streets, the people … grey, sad and unending*. But he found Stalin impressive. *Though I knew the man to be without mercy, I respected the quality of his mind … no one could have been less doctrinaire*. Eden was never to waver in his opinion of Stalin, whom he was to meet several times more during the Second World War. *I have never known a man handle himself better in conference … prudent but not slow, seldom raising his voice, a good listener … he was the quietest dictator I have ever known … Yet the strength was there, unmistakably.*[27]

Eden was feted on this visit. When he visited the Moscow Opera House, the orchestra played the British national anthem and after he toured the underground, a station was named after him. A statement emphasised the two countries' common belief in collective security and the lack of conflict 'on any of the main issues of international policy'. Eden knew, however, that his colleagues would be unenthusiastic because *some regarded communism as anti-Christ*.[28] Here was a second issue that would increasingly divide British politicians: was Soviet Russia beyond the pale as an ally and was her army, in any case, too weak?

Though I knew the man to be without mercy, I respected the quality of his mind … he was the quietest dictator I have ever known … Yet the strength was there, unmistakably.

EDEN ON STALIN

But for the rest of 1935, Mussolini was the centre of attention. He wanted to build a new Roman empire and the ancient kingdom of Abyssinia, which lay between the Italian colonies of Eritrea and Somalia, was an obvious target. He was building up his forces for an invasion. Eden was unable to attend the year's first meeting with the Duce, held in Stresa so that Britain, France and Italy could agree a common front against Germany. On his way back from Moscow, his plane ran into a fierce storm. Eden was ordered *complete rest for six weeks, the heart having been strained*. So MacDonald and Simon went to Stresa without him. They assured Eden they would raise Abyssinia with Mussolini. They didn't and Eden called it *a most unhappy lapse*.[29]

Here was the third issue that would divide the British. Vansittart, in particular, wanted Italy as an ally against Germany. Eden argued that resistance to aggression was indivisible. Abyssinia was a member of the League and to abandon her was to endanger the system of collective security that alone could stop Hitler. Perhaps more importantly, Eden never hit it off with Mussolini, whom he regarded as a bully and *a complete gangster* with bad table manners, while Mussolini called Eden 'the best-dressed fool'. With Hitler, by contrast, Eden could at least have a genial discussion about soldiering, having discovered they fought opposite each other on the Western Front in 1918. For this rather flimsy reason, Eden thought agreements with him might have *a chance of a reasonable life*.[30]

Yet Eden was no clearer than any of his colleagues about how the League should act. *I find it difficult to know what is the next step to take*, read a typical 1935 note.[31] He later criticised his colleagues for lack of firm purpose but, for most of the year, at the very least he went along with them.

At first, Eden seemed to hold the secret of restraining Mussolini. On returning to work in May, he went to Geneva and brokered a deal for the Abyssinian dispute to go to arbitration. Once again, the golden boy had wielded his magic. Haile Selassie, the Abyssinian emperor, thanked him. 'It now looks certain that he will become Foreign Secretary,' wrote the Tory MP Harold Nicolson in his diary. 'How angry all the young Tories will be.'[32] Days later, Eden himself learnt from Hankey, the Cabinet Secretary, *that I was to have the Foreign Office*. Baldwin had now succeeded the ageing MacDonald as premier and was ready for his first reshuffle. Eden had already told him that *I could not, after all these years, usefully play second to a new chief*. Yet within hours of Hankey's assurance, Eden learned that Sir Samuel Hoare, moving from the India Office, was to replace Simon. Eden would stay where he was, but with the added authority of Cabinet membership. He was bitterly disappointed and told Baldwin so. *I felt I knew what was needed in British foreign policy and I could not help realising that the Foreign Office would have been glad to see me appointed.*[33]

Eden initially thought little better of Hoare than he did of Simon, describing him in his diary as *slippery Sam*.[34] Yet two months later, Eden wrote that *happily we see eye to eye in every respect*.[35] Eden made little protest when Hoare sent him to Rome with proposals for a new deal, which would give Mussolini extra territory. But the Duce wanted far more land and said that, if necessary, he would go to war to get it and wipe Abyssinia from the map.

I felt I knew what was needed in British foreign policy and I could not help realising that the Foreign Office would have been glad to see me appointed.

EDEN

This was precisely an example of the secret diplomacy, trying to buy off an aggressor without reference to the League's collective security principles, which Eden supposedly deplored. After Mussolini rejected his overtures, wrote Eden in his memoirs, *the time had come to take a stand*.[36] Yet when Hoare went to Geneva in September to make a rousing and widely acclaimed speech on collective security, Eden worried he had gone too far.

A few weeks later, Italy invaded Abyssinia. The League agreed to impose sanctions. But what form they would take, and whether they would include oil and entail a naval blockade, was left in the air. Sanctions were not necessarily a soft option; they might lead Mussolini to declare war. Hoare warned Eden of 'great perturbation' in the Cabinet that he might go too far in Geneva, and get ahead of the hesitant French. Thus, Hoare, a hawk in September, was a dove in October while Eden seemed to move in the opposite direction. This was a symptom of confusion among the entire Cabinet.

The Hoare-Laval Pact – an episode that caused at the time more outrage than Munich and plunged the government into complete disarray – was therefore a disaster waiting to happen. On his way to a holiday in Switzerland, Hoare stopped in Paris for talks with Laval, now the French premier as well as foreign minister, and a man who during the war was to head the collaborationist government. *Hoare gave no indication, publicly or privately, that he was intending to embark on a serious negotiation*, wrote Eden in his memoirs.[37] This makes the whole thing sound more casual than it was. If Hoare had intended only a social call, he would hardly have taken Vansittart with him; in any case, officials of the two countries' foreign offices had already discussed the outlines of a pact, as Eden must have known.

What emerged from Paris was a draft agreement that Abyssinia should lose between a third and a half of its territory. Eden admitted in his memoirs that he then chose the wrong options. Instead of insisting that the Cabinet recall Hoare from his holiday and tell him immediately to scrap the plan, he, like his colleagues, hesitated. Perhaps Hoare had good reasons for making the agreement which London didn't know about. Perhaps the terms could be amended in Geneva.

Perhaps, if Eden spoke his mind, he would be charged with pique against a man who had been promoted over his head. Eden soft-pedalled his opposition in Cabinet and telegraphed Addis Ababa saying the Emperor should give *careful and favourable consideration* to the proposals.[38]

The public was outraged. Less than a month earlier the government had successfully fought a general election promising that the dictators would be resisted through the League. Now, it was cutting the ground from under the League's feet. The reaction in Geneva, Eden reported when he got there, *was even worse than I had anticipated.*[39] When Hoare eventually returned to London, the denouement was inevitable. He resigned a week before Christmas and Baldwin announced the peace plan was 'absolutely and completely dead'.[40]

The prize he had sought so long was surely now Eden's. Did he still want it? His protestations, then and later, that he didn't want such *a wretchedly disordered heritage* may seem the product of vanity and vacillation. Or perhaps he already sensed that the National Government was on the wrong side of history. *It was now infinitely more difficult to impose an acceptable Abyssinian settlement on Mussolini, even with stricter sanctions*, he recalled. Eden met Baldwin, who went through the options. Austen Chamberlain? Too old. Lord Halifax? He couldn't have a Foreign Secretary in the Lords. *Silence followed. Eventually he... said: 'It looks as if it will have to be you.'... somewhat hurt at this eliminative method of being appointed, I replied that six months before I would have been grateful ... but that now I felt quite differently about it. Baldwin nodded ... and so this strange interview ended with my words being taken as tacit acceptance.*[41] It was perhaps an indication of Eden's brittle mood that, within weeks, he was threatening to resign because he was told that ambassadorial appointments had first to be submitted to the head of the Civil Service.

All the same, at 38, he was the youngest Foreign Secretary since 1851 and the undoubted star of the National Government, admired as much by Labour as by Tory MPs. The *New Statesman* described his appointment as 'the best Christmas present the PM could have given us'. To William Clark, his future press adviser who was then a sixth-former at Oundle, he was a boyhood hero, 'a bright and shining light of hope'.[42] That didn't stop some of his fellow politicians eagerly anticipating his fall. They included the man who would later become almost a second father to him. 'I expect the greatness of his office will find him out,' wrote Churchill to his wife.[43]

Chapter 3: Foreign Secretary: 1936–8

It was perhaps as well that Eden got his promotion; his job as League of Nations minister was redundant. The League was dead as surely as disarmament had been killed off 18 months earlier. The two great hopes for collective security were gone. The only road to peace now was through old-fashioned bilateral treaties and pacts.

Nobody even mentioned the League when Eden faced the first significant crisis in his new position: Hitler's military re-occupation of the Rhineland. At Versailles, Germany had been forced to accept a demilitarised zone on its western borders with France and Belgium. In March 1936, as a taxi-driver put it to Eden, 'Jerry moved troops into his own backyard'. Hitler's excuse was that a Franco-Soviet pact signed the previous May had changed everything. But he had defied not just Versailles but the Treaty of Locarno which Germany had freely signed in 1925 and which was regarded as the bedrock of European peace. Alexander Cadogan, a senior Foreign Office man who later became Permanent Secretary, confided to his diary in 1941 '*that* was the turning point'.[1]

But ministers were then at least as worried about the dangers of French retaliation as about Hitler. Baldwin's fear, according to Cabinet minutes, was that a French victory, if achieved with Russia's aid, 'would probably only result in Germany going Bolshevik'.[2] The French general staff had more or less vetoed military action, but the British didn't know that at the time and strained every sinew to stop the French fighting. Eden was not even angry – just a trifle miffed because he had hoped to use the Rhineland as a bargaining counter in negotiations.

Later, Eden admitted that he should have been *stiffer to Hitler* at this moment.[3] But it is hard to quarrel with the verdict of his memoirs: *There was not one man in a thousand in the country ... prepared to take physical action ... Many ... thought it unreasonable that Germany should not be allowed to do as she wished in her own territory, nearly 20 years after the end of the war.*[4]

Hitler coupled his action with offers to rejoin the League and to make a variety of non-aggression pacts, a perfect example, according to Eden's memoirs, of how he *would accompany each blow with an offer nicely calculated to tempt the victim.*[5] The Cabinet was duly tempted. Within two days, with Eden's agreement, it decided to seek 'as far-reaching and enduring a settlement as possible while Herr Hitler is still in the mood'.[6] Eden thought it important that he persuaded the Cabinet to agree on talks between British, French and Belgian military officers. They lasted five days and then lapsed until 1939.

Many ... thought it unreasonable that Germany should not be allowed to do as she wished in her own territory, nearly 20 years after the end of the war.

EDEN

Less than two months later, Haile Selassie bowed to the inevitable and fled Abyssinia. The King of Italy was proclaimed Emperor of Ethiopia. Eden's colleagues asked if there was any point in continuing sanctions, such as they were. They allowed economic competitors, particularly Germany, to entrench themselves in the Italian market. They drove Mussolini towards Hitler and caused trouble with the French.

Even Eden now seemed to agree; his main concern was that Britain should not appear to take the lead in backing down. By this, he probably meant that Anthony Eden shouldn't appear to take the lead. In June, Neville Chamberlain, the Chancellor of the Exchequer, said publicly that continuing sanctions was 'the very midsummer of madness'. Eden wasn't consulted and Chamberlain apologised. In reality, Eden didn't mind. Sanctions were finished, but his reputation remained intact.

The British response to the invasion of Abyssinia had been a fiasco from start to finish. Eden had certainly wanted a stronger line. *I did not feel called upon to resign*, he later explained, *for I had not had control of policy either in the earlier stages ... or during the critical first period in the imposition of sanctions, when my own decisions would have been more persistent and far-reaching ... Nor would the Abyssinians have remained unarmed if I had had my way.*[7] But the historical record leaves doubt as to whether Eden made 'my way' sufficiently clear, even in his own mind.

Now Mussolini posed questions on a new front. In Spain, civil war had begun, with Nationalist rebels under General Franco threatening an elected Republican government. This war, Eden recalled, *was to fire the imagination of the younger generation in many countries, enlisting the devotion unto death of thousands of true volunteers.*[8] Later, the German and Italian interventions, on Franco's side, were widely seen as a dry run for the Second World War. But for most of 1936 it remained a civil war. The main aim of British policy was to stop it spreading. If there was sympathy for either side, it was for Franco, ministers being anxious that the Republican government would turn into a Bolshevik one, particularly with Stalin giving it open support. Eden inclined more towards the Republicans. But what all ministers hoped was that the subject would go away.

In September 1936, all the main European powers made a non-intervention agreement. The British and French observed it; the Germans, Italians and Russians didn't. In January 1937, Britain and Italy concluded what was laughably called 'a gentleman's agreement' which was supposed to ensure mutual respect for each other's Mediterranean interests. Immediately afterwards, 3,000 Italian troops landed in Cadiz. This, wrote Eden, *taught me a lesson, that there was no value in negotiating with Mussolini again.*[9]

Eden had surely learned that lesson over Abyssinia, and was simply angry that he had allowed himself, or been forced, to forget it. Now, with this humiliation fresh in Eden's mind, a change of British leadership was approaching. Chamberlain became Prime Minister in May 1937. According to Oliver Harvey, Eden's private secretary at the Foreign Office, Eden thought Chamberlain *had the makings of a really great Prime Minister ... he had a grip of affairs which Stanley Baldwin had never had.*[10] *He and I*, Eden wrote later, *were closer to each other than to any other member of the Government, exchanging opinions on many Cabinet matters without any disagreement.* Eden was not at all upset when his new boss said he would take more interest in foreign policy than Baldwin. *We both knew that no one could have taken less*, he wrote.[11]

> General Francisco Franco (1892–1975) defeated the Republicans in Spain in 1939, but despite the help the Axis powers had given him during the Civil War, he kept Spain officially neutral during the Second World War, although a Spanish volunteer force, the Blue Division, did fight on the Eastern Front from 1941 to 1943. He also kept up contacts with the Allies, in 1944 even offering Churchill an Anglo-Spanish alliance against Communism. After the war, the Western Powers courted him as an ally in the Cold War. Thus Franco was the only fascist dictator of the 1930s to survive, to rule Spain until his death in 1975.

Chamberlain is often portrayed in hindsight as a weak, indecisive figure who, as the Labour leader Clement Attlee put it, was like a wireless 'permanently tuned to Midland Regional'. The reality was that, when he came to power, he was the only statesman in western Europe, including Hitler, who had a definite programme. He would remove the grievances on which Hitler fed. Then there would be no need for war, and perhaps no need for Nazism either. As the historian A J P Taylor wrote, he was 'driven by hope, not fear'.[12]

He [Chamberlain] *and I were closer to each other than to any other member of the Government, exchanging opinions on many Cabinet matters without any disagreement.*

EDEN

Chamberlain had no reason to think Eden would oppose his programme. *Nations cannot be expected to incur automatic military obligations save for areas where their vital interests are concerned*, Eden had told his constituents in November 1936.[13] To declare a readiness to fight for Czechs or Austrians, Eden said on another occasion, *would be going far beyond our obligations under the* [League] *Covenant and far beyond where the people of this country were prepared to go.*[14] Moreover, Eden had calmly discussed handing over colonies to Hitler in return for greater European security. Not that Hitler, then or later, showed much practical interest: he had told the *Daily Mail* in 1934 that colonies were 'costly luxuries, even for England'[15] and he exploited Germany's grievances about the loss of her colonies in 1918 only for their propaganda value. But it was Eden who first formed the policy that would lead to Munich: suggesting to Hitler concessions that he hadn't actually demanded.

The break with Chamberlain would come not over appeasement in general or in principle but over how to handle Mussolini. Even here the chief disagreements tended to be over tactics, timing and procedure. Yet the policy difference was important. Chamberlain thought it essential to divide the dictators. The Chiefs of Staff would warn in November 1937, after Germany, Italy and Japan had signed a pact, that Britain could not hope to fight all three simultaneously and it was vital 'to reduce the number of our potential enemies'.[16] Eden did not think the pact would come to much in practice. So much did he distrust Mussolini that he didn't think he could be a reliable ally even to Hitler.

The clearest statement of his position, and how it differed from Chamberlain's, was set out in a November 1937 memorandum. It would be wrong to try to break up the German-Italian-Japanese bloc by offering concessions to any of them, he wrote. *The aims of all three are ... inimical to British interests and a surrender to one might well be the signal for further concerted action on the part of all three powers.* While it might be necessary to acquiesce *in more than one fait accompli*, Britain should not *open the floodgates* by agreeing to *expansion before it occurs*. Chamberlain thought it best to anticipate events and get something in return; Eden thought that, whatever the dictators offered, it wouldn't be worth having. For example, Eden himself initiated moves to recognise officially the Italian conquest of Abyssinia (a *fait accompli* if ever there was one) and, when the New Zealand premier protested that this would be immoral, Eden told him he was *very badly and inadequately informed*.[17] But Eden was willing to grant recognition as a gesture, coupling it with a strengthening of the Anglo-French alliance to deter Mussolini from further adventures. He 'regarded a bargain as too repugnant', recorded Harvey. Chamberlain described it as 'giving away our best card for nothing'.[18]

Given these divisions, Eden understandably preferred to deal with the dictators himself. Maurice Hankey took the rather harsh view that 'at bottom he is vain and doesn't like anyone else to get any credit in Foreign Affairs'.[19] But Eden was surely justified in feeling aggrieved when Chamberlain went behind his back. *Complete confidence and candour between Prime Minister and Foreign Secretary*, he wrote in his memoirs, *are indispensable*.[20] Yet for several months, the two men ran what amounted to separate foreign policies. Chamberlain held meetings with Count Grandi, the Italian ambassador in London, and encouraged Dame Ivy Chamberlain, his sister-in-law, to meet Mussolini in Rome. Eden did not know the full details until years later. He was perhaps also unaware that rival Cabinet ministers, particularly Simon and Hoare, were spreading rumours about his health and mental stability.

The first inkling that all would not go well with Chamberlain came in July 1937. With anti-British propaganda growing in Italy and with Mussolini building up forces in the Mediterranean, Eden told Chamberlain that he would draft a personal letter to the Italian leader. But a few days later, Chamberlain, without consultation, wrote his own note, which Eden described as *very friendly in tone*.[21] Eden's objection, as he wrote to Vansittart, was that while the British should show themselves ready to talk, they should be *in no scrambling hurry to offer incense on a dictator's altar*.[22] This was to be a recurring theme over the next six months – that the British, if they must appease, should not chase after the dictators. This ran directly counter to Chamberlain's brisk, 'get on with the job' attitude. Frequently, he acted because Eden, having seemed to agree to do something, failed to act. As Cadogan, who had by then succeeded Vansittart as FO Permanent Secretary, wrote in his diary: 'A... doesn't like the medicine... but then he seems to agree to take it, and uses every excuse... to run out.'[23]

Eden made little fuss about Chamberlain's July letter. He still had high hopes of Chamberlain, particularly on rearmament. Here, in Eden's view, Baldwin had been too dilatory, and Chamberlain as Chancellor more sympathetic to Eden's demands for more defence spending. Even so, Chamberlain as Prime Minister *clearly had the financial situation much in mind.* Shortly before he left the Treasury, his officials warned that, unless spending was restrained, Britain faced another 1931. A *high priority*, Eden recalled, ... *was placed on the maintenance of our economic stability.*[24]

In fact, both men were wrong on two counts. First, neither understood (and few people did at the time) how rearmament might lead to boom rather than bust. Second, both thought Britain needed time to rearm. Their differences were over the pace of rearmament and over how to handle the dictators in the meantime. But if Britain needed time, so did the Germans, whose leaders thought they would not be ready for war until 1943. Much policy at this time was formed on the basis of exaggerated estimates of German strength. If the *Luftwaffe* had been as formidable as ministers then thought, Britain would never have survived in 1940.

Within a few weeks of the July letter, however, came the first of three incidents that were to make the gulf between Chamberlain and Eden unbridgeable. A crisis over the Sudetenland was brewing. This almost entirely German-speaking area on the Germany-Czech border had been ceded to Czechoslovakia after the war. Many, though not all, of the three million inhabitants wished to join the Reich, and Hitler was encouraging and financing unrest. He was also threatening Austria.

Now Lord Halifax, the Lord Privy Seal, was invited by the Nazi minister Hermann Göring to Berlin for the International Sporting Exhibition. There was a chance he would meet Hitler, and Chamberlain saw it as an ideal opportunity of 'getting together' with the dictator and moving forward on his policy of removing grievances before they threatened open conflict. According to his memoirs, Eden *was not eager, but saw no sufficient reason to oppose* the visit. Halifax's version was that Eden was keener than he was. Eden's view changed when he learnt that Halifax could not meet Hitler in Berlin but would have to go to his eyrie in Berchtesgaden. *I did not think it good ... that we should appear to be running after him.*[25]

Eden's backbone was stiffened by the three men who were closest to him at the Foreign Office: Harvey, his private secretary, Viscount Cranborne, his under-secretary, and Jim Thomas, his PPS. 'You are the only Foreign Secretary in sight,' wrote Harvey. 'If you left the Cabinet, the Government would fall ...you are able to impose your terms.'[26] But when he confronted Chamberlain, Eden, who had flu, was *adjured ... to go home and take an aspirin.*[27] No resignation ensued.

Little came of Halifax's visit, except a delicious story that, on arrival, he had started to hand his hat to Hitler, thinking he was a footman, before the German foreign minister whispered *'Der Führer! Der Führer!'* But as Eden found when he got hold of a record of the meeting, Halifax had spoken of 'possible alterations in the European order which might be destined to come about with the passage of time'.[28] As Eden saw it, Hitler would assume he could continue subversive activities in both the Sudetenland and Austria.

For the rest of 1937, relations between Eden and Chamberlain seemed to improve. In a New Year letter to the Prime Minister, Eden wrote: *I do hope that you will never for an instant feel that any interest you take in foreign affairs, however close, would ever be resented by me.*[29] Perhaps Chamberlain took this literally. A few days later, while Eden was on holiday and Chamberlain in charge of the Foreign Office, 'a most secret communication' from the American president, F D Roosevelt, proposed an international conference 'to agree on the essential principles to be observed in the conduct of international relations'.

Chamberlain, who thought the Americans 'a nation of cads', thought the idea laughable. Without consulting Eden, he sent Roosevelt a discouraging reply.

Chamberlain had some justice on his side. America at this time was resolutely isolationist. Though Japanese aggression continued, the US was not keen to apply either economic or military sanctions. It preferred to express high-minded disapproval, leaving any fighting to others. All Chamberlain could see emerging from a con-ference was a torrent of moral homilies. Hitler and Mussolini would see it as an attempt to put them in the wrong and use it as an excuse to postpone talks with Britain. Chamberlain had high hopes of such talks, particularly those he planned with Mussolini to make a deal in return for *de jure* recognition of Italy's conquest of Abyssinia.

I do hope that you will never for an instant feel that any interest you take in foreign affairs, however close, would ever be resented by me.

EDEN TO CHAMBERLAIN

Eden, on the other hand, would *travel not only from Geneva to Brussels, but from Melbourne to Alaska* to get US participation in an international conference.[30] Solidarity between the world's two most powerful democracies was the best way to bring the dictators to heel. *It is almost impossible*, he would write to Chamberlain, *to overestimate the effect which an indication of United States interest in European affairs may be calculated to produce.*[31] Everything else, thought Eden, should give way. If Roosevelt was against recognition of the Italian regime in Abyssinia – and he had said he was – the whole idea should be dropped immediately.

Eden, alerted by his officials, rushed back from holiday, and went to Chequers to convey these views to Chamberlain. *Our meeting was stiff ... For the first time our relations were seriously at odds.*[32] Resignation was again in the air. 'He can afford to be as firm as he likes as now they realise he will resign on it they are afraid of him,' wrote Harvey in his diary.[33] Once more, however, Eden's nerve failed him. One reason was that, since the Roosevelt proposals were strictly secret, he could not explain publicly his reasons for resignation – though many politicians would easily have found ways round that. At any rate, while he persuaded the Cabinet that a more encouraging response should be sent to Roosevelt, the final draft was still not overly enthusiastic, and it insisted that the British would press ahead with talking to Mussolini.

Roosevelt's proposal came to nothing and, by now, Hitler was moving towards annexation of Austria. He had summoned the Austrian Chancellor and told him that a pro-Nazi minister must be put in control of the police. But again, there was no question of anyone stopping Hitler. Eden, always more accommodating to Hitler than to Mussolini, had told the German ambassador in December that *people in England recognise that a closer connexion between Germany and Austria would have to come about sometime.*[34] This formed the backdrop to the third and final dispute between Eden and Chamberlain. The Prime Minister's view was that Anglo-Italian talks, to which Eden had previously agreed, should go ahead. With the prospect of a heavily-armed Nazi state on his border, Mussolini would be all the more anxious 'to know where he stood with us'.[35] In Eden's view, Mussolini had probably acquiesced in Hitler's actions and *it would be humiliating for us to be talking* at such a time.[36]

Chamberlain and Eden met Grandi to discuss an agenda for talks. Grandi emphasised the need for speed if Britain was to stop Italy moving closer to Germany. Eden recorded: *N.C... . sat there nodding his head approvingly, while Grandi detailed one grievance after another. The more N.C. nodded the more outrageous became Grandi's account until ... it would almost seem that* we *had invaded Abyssinia*. After Grandi left, Chamberlain said talks should start immediately in Rome. When Eden demurred, saying once more that Britain shouldn't chase after the dictators, *Chamberlain became... more vehement than I have ever seen him, and strode up and down the room saying... 'Anthony, you have missed chance after chance. You simply cannot go on like this.'*[37] Grandi reported

It cannot be in the country's interest that those who are called upon to direct its affairs should work in an uneasy partnership.

EDEN TO CHAMBERLAIN

to Rome that Eden and Chamberlain had been 'like two cocks in true fighting posture'. Chamberlain recorded: 'I knew ... I must make my final stand and that Anthony must yield or go.'[38]

Despite several more meetings, including a day of Cabinet meetings, Eden could not flinch a third time. Simon said: 'You look rather ill. Are you certain that you're all right?' Later, Simon told Jim Thomas that he should take Eden away for six months on holiday. Halifax, after visiting Eden and his team at the Foreign Office, found 'whisky & sodas, & cigarettes' and an atmosphere like 'the corner of a boxing ring when the seconds received back the pugilist and restored his vitality by congratulations and encouragement'.[39]

In the Cabinet, only four of Eden's 18 colleagues gave him even qualified support. Several said they had, as Halifax put it, 'no intimation of this alleged fundamental difference' and were naturally baffled that an argument over the timing and location of talks should have led to resignation. No Cabinet minister followed him out of office and Malcolm MacDonald, who might have done, felt he could 'scarcely break up the National Government on so small an issue'.[40]

But resignations often occur over a detail, which is merely the culmination of several disagreements caused by more fundamental issues. *It cannot be in the country's interest*, Eden wrote to Chamberlain, *that those who are called upon to direct its affairs should work in an uneasy partnership.*[41] Vansittart thought it a mistake to resign on an issue 'which would be difficult to explain to the country'.[42] Yet though they may not have understood the precise issues, the public supported Eden; 71 per cent thought he was right to resign, according to Gallup the following month. In the sense that the issue was Mussolini, it was the right issue. Like Eden, the public hated Mussolini, who had destroyed the League of Nations, more than they hated Hitler.

Churchill, lamenting the loss of this 'one strong young figure' lay sleepless all night 'consumed by emotions of sorrow and fear'. Harvey heard of an Austrian servant found weeping 'because Mr Eden has resigned and she didn't know now what would become of her mother who was a Jewess in Vienna'. 'The Socialists,' a pro-appeasement Tory noted sourly in his diary, 'now proclaim Eden as their savour and leader.' At parties in Rome, the news was greeted with cheering and toasting. At the Foreign Office, Halifax, of whom it was said 'he looked his best astride a horse', asked if it would still be possible for him to hunt on Saturdays. Duly reassured, he agreed to be Eden's successor.[43]

Chapter 4: Munich and the 'Phoney War': 1938–40

Shortly after his resignation, Eden wrote to Halifax from Yorkshire that *the moors in this glorious weather do not ... encourage me to contemplate a return to political life, ever.*[1] All the same, many, particularly his old mentor Baldwin, still considered Eden the eventual successor to Chamberlain. It was with this in mind that Baldwin prompted him to broaden his authority on domestic affairs by touring the depressed areas that summer, including Tyneside, Wales and Glasgow. As late as April 1939, a poll found that 38 per cent of the public backed Eden to become PM, with his chief rivals, Halifax and Churchill, getting only 7 per cent each. Yet by the time Chamberlain resigned in May 1940, Eden was out of the running.

The main reason was that Eden, whether out of party loyalty, hopes of a swift return or underlying sympathy for the principles of Chamberlain's policies, declined to take any leadership role in the Tory backbench opposition. Harvey, though still in the Foreign Office, stayed close to Eden and his diaries repeatedly record him planning to step up his criticisms of the government. But he never did so, proving as pusillanimous on this as he had on resignation. He made a bland resignation speech to the Commons and, in the ensuing debate, according to Duff Cooper, one of Eden's sympathisers in the

Cabinet who was himself to resign later in the year, 'one could feel opinion veering steadily towards the Government'.[2]

Eden had little or nothing to say about Hitler's annexation of Austria in March 1938, about the early stages of the Sudeten crisis that was to take Britain to the brink of war in September, or even about the conclusion of the Anglo-Italian agreement (preparations for which had prompted his resignation) in April. Speculation that he might quickly return to the government never went away and many thought he was just currying favour. According to Harvey, 'he has to be careful not to get into a position of becoming a symbol for war on dictatorship'.[3] Churchill was the war symbol, and Eden kept his distance from him, presiding over a separate group of Tory dissenters known as 'the Eden group' or by its detractors, as 'the glamour boys'. Yet Eden was the greater potential danger to the government, closer to the political centre ground and more widely admired among Opposition politicians than Churchill, who was regarded as a maverick right-winger. Eden's failure to land any punches on Chamberlain exasperated his potential allies. 'What is the bloody fellow doing?' asked Labour's Hugh Dalton. By September, a former Conservative MP was warning him: 'Your stock has fallen appreciably.'[4]

As the crisis over Czechoslovakia grew, and Chamberlain flew to Germany to confront Hitler, Churchill demanded an explicit ultimatum to the *Führer* and even travelled to Paris to try and rally the French. Eden confined himself to private messages to Halifax and a letter to the *Times* which stated that *it should not be impossible to evolve ... a settlement acceptable to all*. By the last week of September, war seemed inevitable. At a meeting with Chamberlain at Godesburg, Hitler demanded that his troops should occupy those areas that had a majority of German speakers. Halifax – partly because of

Eden's private entreaties – persuaded the Cabinet to resist. The fleet was mobilised and in British cities people tried on gas masks.

During a Commons debate on 27 September, however, a scrap of paper was passed along the government front bench. Chamberlain rose to announce that Hitler had invited Mussolini, the French premier Edouard Daladier and himself to another meeting in Munich. *Members of all parties rose to their feet, cheered and waved their order papers*, wrote Eden. *I did not feel I could take part in this scene, neither did Churchill.*[5] However, when Churchill drafted a telegram to Chamberlain imploring him to make no more concessions, Eden and other supposed anti-appeasers declined to sign. Churchill, according to one account, was left 'sitting ... immobile, frozen, like a man of stone' with 'tears in his eyes'.[6]

Members of all parties rose to their feet, cheered and waved their order papers. I did not feel I could take part in this scene, neither did Churchill.

EDEN

At Munich, Chamberlain and Daladier agreed to what were in effect the Godesburg terms, though they were more plausibly dressed up. The Czechs had no say in the matter. After the meeting, Chamberlain got Hitler to sign a declaration of 'the desire of our two peoples never to go to war with one another again'. On his return to London, Chamberlain waved this piece of paper, announcing 'peace in our time'.

In his memoirs, Eden accepted that Munich could be defended *as the price to be paid for a military weakness*. There was no excuse, however, for believing Hitler had been finally bought off. *When the first relief at being spared a total war had passed away, the British people would have been more than ever ready to make sacrifices if the issues had been explained to them. No firm leadership and no sufficient acceleration in our defence preparations were forthcoming.*[7]

In Eden's view, Chamberlain failed to provide firm leadership. But some thought Eden himself was just as culpable. In the Commons debate on Munich, he and Churchill both abstained, but the latter made by far the more stirring speech. Eden praised Chamberlain for *the sincerity and pertinacity which he has devoted ... to averting the supreme calamity of war*.[8] His friends were disappointed, even shocked. Harvey now pressed him to 'beat a drum rather than play a piano'. Harold Nicolson complained that 'the whole youth of the country is waiting for a stirring lead' but all Eden did was 'to repeat flabby formulas'.[9] When, shortly after Munich, Eden visited America, he was cheered on the streets as though he were a Hollywood star. 'He is St George fighting the dragons,' gushed one American newspaper. Yet his chief anxiety, it seems, was to convince the Americans that Chamberlain and the Cabinet were not as pro-fascist as they looked. Eden's fear perhaps was that Chamberlain would call an election on the back of Munich, a sort of 'khaki election' in reverse. He might then have to consider standing as an independent Conservative, and risk losing his seat. And for a time, Munich seemed a success. In March 1939, Chamberlain told the press that Europe was settling down to a period of tranquillity.

A few days later, Hitler marched into Prague. A month later, Mussolini invaded Albania without warning. The British ambassador in Rome lodged a 'protest' so conciliatory in tone that the Italian Foreign Minister wrote that it 'might have been composed in our own offices'. This, judged Eden, was *the nadir of ... appeasement*.[10] Yet still, in a Commons speech, he failed to put the knife in, and got a grateful note from Chamberlain as a result.

Eden was now keener than ever on returning to the government, partly because with appeasement so obviously discredited the gap between him and Chamberlain was narrowing.

But Chamberlain was still afraid of further provoking the dictators, sending them 'off the deep end', as the junior minister Lord Dunglass (the future Prime Minister Sir Alec Douglas-Home) put it. When Eden offered to go and meet Stalin in order to push forward negotiations for a Soviet alliance, Chamberlain vetoed the idea. Given the rapport he had earlier established with Stalin, it is just possible that it was Eden, after all, who could have averted war. A British-French-Soviet pact might have stopped Hitler in his tracks. Instead, Hitler signed his own pact with Stalin which, by giving him a free military hand in Poland, made war virtually inevitable. After Munich, Britain and France had given firm guarantees to Poland. Appeasement had run its course.

Not that Chamberlain didn't still try to wriggle off the hook and Eden still keep his head down. In the Commons debate on 2 September, the day after Hitler had invaded Poland, it was left to another Tory anti-appeaser, Leo Amery, to shout the famous words 'speak for England, Arthur' when Arthur Greenwood, the Labour deputy leader, rose to insist there must be no second Munich. Chamberlain broadcast to the nation the next day, announcing that Hitler had failed to withdraw his troops from Poland and war had therefore started. To Eden, it *seemed rather like the lament of a man deploring his own failure than the call of a nation of arms*. If Eden himself had been more willing to issue calls to arms, he might have been in a stronger position to negotiate his position in a reconstructed government. He had to be included because Churchill – whose recruitment to the Cabinet was now politically essential – insisted on it. But he was offered the relatively lowly position of Secretary of State for Dominion Affairs. Despite being so recently a prospective premier, he did not even have a seat in the War Cabinet, though he could attend its meetings. Eden did not like this *highly anomalous, not to say humiliating* position.[11] But his country was at war, and he could do no other.

The next eight months were a strange period, during which the men of Munich, headed by Chamberlain, were still in power, a negotiated peace was constantly talked about (at the end of 1939, a Cabinet Office civil servant rated the chances at 50–50), and rumours circulated that Hitler had terrifying new weapons, some involving chemical or biological agents. Hitler overran Poland and the Soviets invaded Finland. But Italy, Japan, the US and even Belgium had still not entered the war, and there was no action on the Western Front.

Eden's job was more important than it sounded because the support of the Dominions, in manpower and materials, was to prove vital. Eden set about the job with his usual zeal and established the successful Empire Air Training Scheme, under which thousands of pilots and navigators from Britain and the Dominions were trained in Canada. But there was no disguising Eden's sense that he was *only on the fringes*.[12] At one stage, it seemed he might go to the War Office, but Chamberlain, who clearly had Eden in the government only on sufferance, vetoed the idea. To many, Eden seemed a diminished figure. After hearing him in the Commons, Dunglass observed that 'it was difficult to realise one was listening to a speech by a man who had been Foreign Secretary'.[13]

Even with Churchill, now First Lord of the Admiralty, his relations were cool. Eden's portfolio included Eire, whose neutrality he strove to make as benevolent to Britain as possible. Churchill, however, wanted to seize the Irish ports. 'A.E.' recorded Harvey, 'is beginning to doubt whether Churchill could ever be P.M. so bad is his judgment in such matters.'[14] Perhaps Eden was miffed that Churchill was clearly getting on better with Chamberlain than he was. The feelings were mutual. Churchill allegedly said in February 1940 that he would rather have Chamberlain than Eden as Prime Minister 'by 8 to 1'. Even so, Churchill continued to press Eden's case for promotion, if only because he was one of his few potential allies in the government.

The 'Phoney War', as it was known, ended in April, when Hitler invaded Denmark and Norway. British forces were landed but had to be evacuated almost immediately. The Commons debated this disaster in early May. Again, Amery's words would ring down the years: 'in the name of God, go!' he told the government, echoing Cromwell. The government majority was cut from 231 to 81, with 41 Conservatives voting against and 60 abstaining. Chamberlain resigned and Labour and the Liberals were invited to join a coalition government. After slight hesitation in the corridors of power, Churchill became its head.

As Hitler advanced on France through Holland and Belgium, Eden got the War Office, though still without a Cabinet seat. Churchill himself was Minister of Defence, as he would remain throughout the war. *I told Mr Churchill that I would do as he asked, but I knew that ... the state of the army was inglorious.* Indeed it was, with equipment in desperate shortage. When Dominions ministers had visited British

I told Mr Churchill that I would do as he asked, but I knew that ... the state of the army was inglorious.

EDEN

forces in France the previous November, one had observed that 'the Germans will go through there like a knife through butter'.[15] The last whimpers of appeasement were still audible in Churchill's early Cabinets. A proposal to approach Mussolini about holding a peace conference was not entirely ruled out until the Duce joined the war on Hitler's side.

But Eden, as war minister, characteristically set about

waging war single-mindedly. His went on the radio and announced the formation of 'the Local Defence Volunteers', later known as the Home Guard, to resist a German invasion. The response, he recalled, *was overwhelming, the first recruit arriving within four minutes of the end of the broadcast.*[16] Though Eden got the historical credit – his broadcast opened the film version of *Dad's Army* more than three decades later – the plans existed at the War Office before he got there and Churchill insisted on the name change, partly because he thought the word 'local' uninspiring.

The BBC television comedy series *Dad's Army* ran between 1968 and 1977, for a total of 80 episodes. It followed the adventures of the Warmington-on-Sea Home Guard platoon, commanded by Captain Mainwaring (played by Arthur Lowe). The series regularly tops polls of viewers' favourite television comedies and is frequently repeated. The feature film, in which Eden's broadcast setting up the Local Defence Volunteers features, was made in 1971 with almost all the original TV cast. Many episodes were recorded for BBC radio, and there was a stage spin-off of the series that played from 1975 to 1976.

Here was an early example of Churchill's somewhat capricious eye for detail – another early instruction to Eden was to restore officers' leather shoulder-straps – and his determination to get his own way. Quite frequently, Eden resisted him. Sometimes he was successful, sometimes not, as over the Home Guard. Churchill could be tetchy and resentful of criticism and even his wife warned him early in the war of his effect on colleagues. *We talked till after 1 am*, Eden noted of a night in September 1940 (late hours chewing the fat being typical of Churchill). *He told me that I ought not to be so violent with him for he was only trying to help me.*[17] Yet in the years to come these two men, so different in age, political views and working habits but also so similar in their vanity, became very close.

Within weeks of the new government taking office, it faced a military rout in France. The evacuation of the British Expeditionary Force from Dunkirk, saving men but little heavy equipment, has gone down in history as a triumph but Eden, the minister in charge, admitted that it was really *an admission of overwhelming defeat for the allies*. Shortly afterwards, Eden and Churchill visited the French army headquarters in the Loire. *We left*, the former recalled, *... with the certainty that effective resistance could not last much longer. As I flew low over Brittany, hedge-hopping above the lovely French countryside in June, I ... wondered whether I should ever see this land again.*[18]

By the end of June, the French, under new leadership, had agreed an armistice with Germany. Now, with an invasion expected daily, Eden visited Kent, Sussex and Surrey, finding not a single anti-tank gun, never mind a tank. He and Sir John Dill, newly appointed by Eden as Chief of the Imperial General Staff, agreed that, with Hitler in control of the Continent, *it was in North Africa that our fighting must be done*.[19] But there too the deficiencies in equipment were shocking. This was the first significant area of difference with Churchill. North Africa and the Middle East were vital: if Britain could control this area then, given her dominance at sea, her supplies were relatively safe while Hitler's supplies of oil and raw materials could be restricted. Churchill, however, did not, as Eden put it, entirely understand *the modern maintenance problems of motor transport, tanks and aircraft, operating in a country of desert space and devoid of industrial capacity*. Churchill persistently singled out General Sir Archibald Wavell, the Middle East commander, for criticism, claiming that he lacked 'mental vigour'. Wavell himself was exasperated by Churchill's attempts to micro-manage, moving *this battalion here and that battalion there.*[20] At one stage, Eden and Dill (whom Churchill didn't like either) threatened resignation unless Wavell was treated better.

Understandably, Churchill at first wanted to conserve equipment for the Home Front. But after the Battle of Britain had been won in the summer, an Italian invasion of Greece quickly followed. Churchill said 'the Greek situation must now be held to dominate others'. In his diary, Eden described this as *strategic folly.* He added: *If we had ever thought to help Greece, we should long since have laid our plans accordingly.*[21] But the end of Eden's seven-month spell at the War Office was approaching. A reluctant Halifax was coaxed out of the Foreign Office and sent to the Washington embassy. Just before Christmas 1940, Eden returned to his old department and was at last in the War Cabinet. Churchill compared it to 'moving up from the fourth form to the sixth' and, as Eden saw it, *my responsibility must be greater as Churchill's colleague at the Foreign Office, than as his subordinate with the army.* (Clearly, he took literally the official doctrine of British cabinet government that the Prime Minister is merely first among equals.) In wartime, Eden added, *diplomacy is strategy's twin.*[22]

In the long term, this may have been true, but it is doubtful that Eden himself believed it at the time. In the early part of the war, as Cadogan noted, 'with our military weakness and the sensational ineptitude of our commanders, diplomacy is completely hamstrung'.[23] Eden would have preferred to be Minister of Defence, the position that Churchill hogged for himself. Throughout the war, the Prime Minister made military decisions with the Chiefs of Staff, excluding Cabinet colleagues whenever he could. Meanwhile, the home front, with its vital tasks of organising the economy and the labour force, was left largely to Labour ministers.

Though Attlee was formally deputy premier from 1942,

Eden was to be Churchill's closest wartime colleague. And as Eden carefully noted each time, the Prime Minister said he did not intend to continue after the war and had designated Eden his successor. Churchill, well aware of the need to flatter his vanity, lost no opportunity to emphasise their closeness, sometimes describing him as 'my son', at other times as 'my right arm'. All the same, we may wonder whether Churchill wanted a more pliant and less prominent figure at the War Office and deliberately kept Eden away from what were then the most important areas of decision-making.

Chapter 5: Wartime Foreign Secretary: 1941–5

Certainly, Eden was restless for much of his first year back at the Foreign Office. He grumbled to his diary that the Foreign Office was *only a bureaucratic machine, gently ticking over*.[1] Harvey, who returned as his private secretary in July, found that 'he longs again for Army or W.O'.[2]

This febrile mood may help explain his first major venture after his return to the FO – a venture that was to end in disaster. Despite his earlier opposition to helping the Greeks, Eden now swung to Churchill's view. Greece was one of the countries to which Chamberlain had issued guarantees in April 1939, after it became clear that appeasement had failed. Though the Italians had been driven back, it was now menaced by Hitler who was advancing through the Balkans. *If another country to which we had given ... a pledge were to fall to the Axis powers without a real effort to prevent it*, wrote Eden, *the effect, especially in the United States, must be deplorable.*[3] But Cadogan felt that a British expedition to Greece '*must*, in the end, be a failure ... A. has rather jumped us into this'.[4]

Eden set off on a tour of the region, including Cairo, Athens and Ankara. It was among many journeys that Eden made during the war and, like several others, it proved hazardous and uncomfortable. At one stage, in terrible weather, with fuel running short, the pilot warned they might have to land at sea or even in Spain (neutral but fascist), where they would probably have been interned. *It was a queer sensation*, Eden wrote, *sitting trussed in one's lifebelt and contemplating the alternatives of internment or drowning.*[5] Cadogan described it as a 'stunt trip' which threatened 'a diplomatic and strategic blunder of the first order'.[6] Eden hoped British action would prompt both Turkey and Yugoslavia to join the war on the Allied side, but there was little prospect of either doing so. In Cairo, Eden persuaded Wavell, whose forces had achieved a string of victories over the Italians in Libya, that he could now spare men and equipment to help Greece, even though, as Wavell's chief of staff later testified, 'all the military evidence was absolutely against'.[7] Perhaps Wavell felt obliged to co-operate because at the War Office Eden had saved his job. In any case, Wavell was still smarting from Churchill's accusations of excessive caution. When Eden moved on to Athens, he ran 'rather ahead of his instructions' in Cadogan's view and made commitments that were almost impossible for the British to reverse. Oliver Stanley, who had been moved from the War Office to make way for Eden in 1940, commented

Erwin Rommel (1891–1944) was Hitler's favourite military commander for most of the war, largely because he had no ties to the old Prussian aristocratic high command, which Hitler always distrusted. Appointed to command a panzer division in the French campaign in 1940, he went on to command the Afrika Korps, where his successes against larger and better-equipped British forces made him famous on both sides of the conflict. Although not directly involved in the July 1944 plot to kill Hitler, his enemies in the high command were able to turn Hitler against him and he was forced to kill himself in 1944. (See *Rommell: The End of a Legend* by Ralf Georg Reath, published by Haus.)

sourly that he had been 'cheered in the streets and smothered in roses'. How, in such circumstances, 'could he keep his judgment clear?'[8] The result was catastrophe, not only in the Balkans but also in North Africa. Most of the 62,000 British troops put ashore in Greece had to be withdrawn almost as soon as they landed, with huge losses of equipment. In North Africa, Hitler sent the Afrika Korps under General Erwin Rommel to reverse Wavell's earlier victories. By April 1941, Eden had to confront the possibility of *the worst calamity*: that the Allies would lose control of Egypt, *the base upon which everything depends*.[9]

In his memoirs, Eden argued that, by engaging the Germans in Greece, the British had forced Hitler to postpone Operation Barbarossa, his planned invasion of the Soviet Union, by five weeks. This delay, he insisted, ultimately led to the Germans being trapped in the Russian winter. But many historians dispute this view and argue Eden's venture was as foolish as it seemed at the time. Eden's enemies sniffed blood. He didn't help himself in the Commons debate on the subject: the backbench Tory Henry Channon had 'never heard an important speech so badly delivered'.[10] Eden's career was saved by Churchill's support, though even he had momentary doubts. Wavell was not so lucky and was soon relieved of his command.

Eden's second big project of 1941– to get the Russians onside – was more successful, though some may think the long-term results were equally questionable. He learnt of the Nazi attack on the Soviet Union at Chequers on 22 June when a valet appeared in his bedroom with a large cigar on a silver salver and a message from Churchill. The two men immediately decided the Soviets should have all possible help, military and economic, and they should be reassured there was no chance of Britain responding to any peace overtures from Hitler. For years, both nations had tried to appease Hitler largely for fear that he would make terms with the other and launch an attack. Now, at last, they were on the same side. Mutual suspicion, however, was not over and many thought the Russians could not resist Hitler for more than a few weeks.

For the next two years and more, Eden was to be the Russians' biggest friend in the Cabinet. *I was determined to do business with the Kremlin despite its communist carapace*, he recalled.[11] Stalin's demands – for men and materials, for a second front against Hitler in western or southern Europe, for recognition of the territorial gains he had made while he had his pact with the Nazis – came thick and fast. Eden could meet only some of them, but he always fought the Soviet Union's corner, while Churchill in particular remained instinctively anti-Bolshevik and Labour ministers were if anything more paranoid about Communism than the Tories.

Since Britain's capacity to help Russia materially was limited, the tendency was to placate Stalin by making diplomatic concessions. For example, Eden pressed the case for declaring war on Finland, in solidarity with Stalin, who had invaded that country in 1939–40. The Cabinet reluctantly agreed, as it also did to declarations of war on Hungary and Romania. In December 1941, however, Eden travelled to Moscow with the offer of what Harvey called 'a big packet of machines' including 500 aircraft and 200 tanks. In the view of one FO official, it was a foolish visit. 'He cannot achieve very much ... Not at all good for Foreign Secretaries to go wandering round in wartime.'[12]

The difficulties became greater when Churchill telephoned during his journey to tell him of the Japanese attack on the American naval base at Pearl Harbor. On the face of it, this was marvellous news because at last it brought the US into the war. *I could not conceal my relief*, recalled Eden.... . *I felt that whatever happened now, it was merely a question of time.* Moreover, Germany and Italy enormously assisted Britain and Russia by quickly, under the terms of a pact with Japan, declaring war on America. If they had not done so, the Americans might have confined their efforts to the Pacific. *Loyalty is not a word commonly associated with Hitler and Mussolini*, observed Eden. *This unique occasion ... sealed their fate.*[13] In the short term, however, Britain had to fight on another front, defending its imperial possessions in the Far East. Eden could not now offer aircraft to Stalin; they were needed to protect Malaya. The focus therefore shifted back to diplomatic concessions. By now, the Germans were only 19 miles from Moscow and it may have seemed to some that Stalin was negotiating from a position of weakness. But the British still feared he might make a separate peace with Hitler.

Stalin proposed a secret protocol which would see the post-war absorption of the Baltic states into the Soviet Union, significant Soviet gains in Hungary, Bulgaria, Finland and Romania, and the extension of Russia's boundaries into Poland with the latter acquiring East Prussia from a defeated Germany as compensation. Eden told Stalin that he could not agree without first consulting his Cabinet colleagues, to say nothing of the US and the Dominions. Stalin reluctantly accepted this and, with the German army *so near that their gunfire was almost within sound*, the meeting concluded with what Eden recorded as an *almost embarrassingly sumptuous* Kremlin banquet which lasted until 5 a.m. and included 36 toasts.[14]

On his return to London, Eden proposed the UK should agree to recognise most of Russia's 1941 frontiers which,

I could not conceal my relief, ... I felt that whatever happened now, it was merely a question of time.

EDEN AFTER PEARL HARBOR

as Churchill put it, 'were acquired by acts of aggression in shameful collusion with Hitler'. The Prime Minister, as Halifax noted, was 'greatly surprised with Anthony' and argued that 'the transfer of the people of the Baltic States to Soviet Russia against their will would be contrary to all the principles for which we are fighting this war'.[15] Eden's reply was that, in reality, nobody could hope to reverse Soviet gains if the war against Hitler was won. *Russia's position on the European continent will be unassailable*, he told the Cabinet. *Russian prestige will be so great that the establishment of Communist Governments in the majority of European countries will be greatly facilitated.*[16] It was therefore best to tie Stalin to agreements while he was at his weakest. The argument became fierce and the parallels were obvious. 'It is curious that A., of all people, should have hopes of "appeasement"!!' wrote Cadogan in his diary.[17] Some thought conceding the Baltic states to Stalin would be even worse than Munich since that agreement at least had the excuse that it was mostly ethnic Germans who were handed over to German rule. Simon, now the Lord Chancellor, warned that he could not defend it in the House of Lords. Even the pro-Soviet Harvey warned: 'He must not get into the position of being the Red Eden.'[18]

The Cabinet insisted the treaty should include a measure of autonomy for the Baltic states and an exit option for citizens who did not wish to live under Soviet rule. Perhaps reaching conclusions similar to Eden's – that nobody could turn them out of the Baltic states in any case – the Russians then decided they could do without an agreement on frontiers. The eventual treaty, in May 1942, merely agreed a 20-year post-war alliance against German aggression. Stalin now rated a wartime second front as more urgent.

But the military situation made a second front unthinkable. The early months of 1942 were, in some respects, even worse for Britain than 1940. The Japanese overran Malaya, the Philippines, Singapore, the Dutch East Indies (later Indonesia) and Burma. By midsummer, Rommel was near the gates of Alexandria and the Nile Delta. In Russia, the German summer offensive penetrated further than in the previous year. 'For the first time,' wrote Harvey, 'the possibility that we may be defeated has come to many people.'[19] Did the blame lie at the top? Many thought it did, and Eden himself shared concerns about Churchill's leadership. In April 1942, he told Cranborne (now Lord Cecil): *I am much troubled about present methods of conducting the war... Brilliant improvisation is no substitute for carefully planned dispositions.*[20] With Churchill's health also in question, his fall seemed a real possibility, and in July he faced a confidence vote in the Commons in which he might have got into deeper trouble had one of his main Tory critics not proposed, to wide hilarity, that the Duke of Gloucester should take command of the Army. Despite some support for Labour's Stafford Cripps, Eden was the most likely candidate to replace him. But he refused to plot against Churchill. 'A.E. said he would do nothing against Winston, now or ever,' recorded Harvey. ' ... I took him to task for this rather passive attitude ... his critics said he wouldn't lead and he was weak and imprecise.'[21] Eden's position may not have been entirely disinterested. He knew that, in mid-June, Churchill had put in writing to George VI that Eden should be his successor, a move for which there was and is no constitutional parallel.

By late autumn, the worst was over. Rommel was driven back and General Bernard Montgomery won the Battle of El Alamein in North Africa. Churchill ordered the church

'A.E. said he would do nothing against Winston, now or ever ... his critics said he wouldn't lead and he was weak and imprecise.'

OLIVER HARVEY

bells to be rung and told the nation, in one of his greatest broadcasts, that it was the end of the beginning, though not the beginning of the end. His position was never seriously threatened again during the war and Eden's hopes of the premiership now rested on either a peacetime succession or a breakdown in Churchill's health.

Churchill remained a difficult colleague, forever poking his nose into what Eden regarded as other people's business. Much of the time, Churchill, not Eden, ran Anglo-American relations and this may partly explain Eden's anxiety to make a success of the Soviet alliance, though Churchill sometimes corresponded privately even with Stalin. It was, Eden grumbled, *just like Neville Chamberlain again*.[22] In November 1942, Churchill appointed him Leader of the House of Commons in addition to his existing job. Given how highly he was regarded by Labour MPs, the appointment was a good one. But the dual role meant, as Eden put it, *a ruthless burning of the candle at both ends*,[23] and it is hard to avoid the suspicion that Churchill hoped it would leave space for himself to play a greater role in foreign policy.

General (later Field Marshal) Bernard Law Montgomery (1887–1976) took command of the Eighth Army in the Western Desert in 1942, and in September and October of that year defeated the German and Italian forces at the battles of Alam Halfa and El Alamein. The first major British land victories of the war, these battles secured Egypt and the Suez Canal, and from then on the Axis forces in North Africa were in retreat until their final surrender in Tunisia on 13 May 1943. Montgomery later took the Eighth Army on to Sicily, before moving to command in France and the Low Countries after D-Day in 1944.

The biggest breach between Churchill and Eden – the one that came nearest to causing the latter to leave the government – would come over Charles de Gaulle, the prickly leader of the Free French. Eden found de Gaulle *a most difficult creature to deal with*.[24] But for the most part, with his diplomat's training, he took a more placatory attitude than either Churchill or Roosevelt. As he saw it, the Americans didn't want France restored as a great power and hoped, after the war, for a more subservient French leadership than de Gaulle was likely to provide. Eden's own policy was best summed up by Roosevelt: 'to build up France into a first-class power which would be on Britain's side.'[25]

Before the winter of 1942, de Gaulle had already quarrelled several times with the Allies, notably over an invasion of Madagascar – a French colony controlled by the collaborationist Vichy regime – of which he was not informed in advance. Now came a far bigger crisis. In November, Anglo-American forces landed in Vichy-controlled northwest Africa. The US military recognised Admiral Darlan, a Vichy naval commander, as the effective controller of the region. In return, he delivered an immediate ceasefire by Vichy supporters and promised (though this he could not ultimately deliver) the French fleet to the Allied side. De

The Vichy French regime controlled Southern France and most of the overseas empire, including North Africa, after the Armistice with the Germans in 1940. Great Britain had attacked the Vichy-controlled fleet at Mers-el-Kébir on 3 July 1940 to prevent it falling into German hands, invaded Vichy-held Syria in 1941 and Madagascar in 1942. The USA, on the other hand, sought to win over Vichy to the Allied cause, as it controlled stronger forces and more territory than the Free French. Given the hostility between Britain and Vichy France, American forces spearheaded the Operation Torch landings in North Africa, as it was thought more likely that the French commanders there would come over to them than the British.

Gaulle was furious, as were many Britons. 'How can we work with Darlan who is a traitor?' asked Harvey.[26] Eden warned Churchill that quislings across Europe would take heart. But Churchill, as usual, took the Americans' side. In his view, de Gaulle left 'a trail of anglophobia' wherever he went; he was 'animated by dictatorial instincts and consumed by personal ambition'. Besides, he told Eden firmly, 'my whole system is based on friendship with Roosevelt'.[27] The crisis was unexpectedly defused on Christmas Eve by Darlan's assassination. *I have not felt so relieved by any event for years*, wrote Eden in his diary.[28]

But the issue of France's future and de Gaulle's role in it did not go away. Churchill, visiting Washington in May 1943, cabled back to London that the time had come to drop de Gaulle. The War Cabinet, rallied by Eden, opposed him. The arguments became even fiercer when the French Committee of National Liberation was formed under de Gaulle in Algiers on 3 June. Eden wanted to recognise the committee as the legitimate government of France, which would rule the country after liberation, pending elections. Roosevelt was adamantly opposed and again Churchill backed him. 'P.M. is being unbelievably tiresome ... A.E. is fed up,' recorded Harvey's diary.[29] Eden set out his position in a formal paper. After the war, he argued, *we are likely to have to work more closely with France even than with the United States... our... policy must aim at the restoration of the independence of the smaller European Allies and of the greatness of France.*[30] 'I will fight you to the death,' Churchill replied. Exactly who blinked first is disputed. 'A reconciliation!' wrote Harvey. 'I'm beginning to know the form now. Frightful row, nervous exhaustion on both sides, then next day a rather contrite P.M. seeking to make up.'[31] Though probably a faithful record of what Eden told his private secretary, this may have been an over-statement. Eden did not get immediate British recognition of de Gaulle's committee, though he got his way soon after.

Perhaps it was as well for Eden's future career that this argument reached its peak a month after another issue had been resolved. For several weeks in the spring of 1943, Eden gave serious thought to becoming Viceroy of India. This was a curious episode, but not as curious as it sounds now. The viceroyalty was then a prestigious position, which involved ruling a fifth of the human race, and Eden loved the idea of *a show of my own*. Besides, noted Harvey, 'he says he is exhausted and will be dead in three months if he has to go on like this'. But Harvey felt, probably rightly, that he would lose his chances of the premiership: 'A.E. is now set for the highest position and he threatens to run out.' Churchill dithered, as did Eden who even asked his detective for his opinion. As Harvey put it, 'he fondly believes ... a grateful country... will summon him back to take over in two or three years' time'.[32] In the end, George VI all but vetoed the idea, and Wavell got the job. No doubt Churchill was tempted by the opportunity to grab the Foreign Secretaryship for himself and may have regretted that he didn't when the two men later quarrelled over the French.

'I'm beginning to know the form now. Frightful row, nervous exhaustion on both sides, then next day a rather contrite P.M. seeking to make up.'

HARVEY ON EDEN AND CHURCHILL

Churchill's growing interest in foreign policy was understandable. The military news was improving all the time – Mussolini fell in July 1943 after Allied landings in Sicily – and questions about the post-war settlement were moving to the forefront. In October 1943, Eden went to Moscow for another conference, with the Americans also attending. Here, plans for the post-war division of Germany and for the United Nations were discussed. As so often, observers praised Eden's role. General Hastings Ismay, chief of staff to the Minister of Defence (who was still Churchill), wrote: 'He never went to a meeting without making sure that he had every aspect of the problem at his fingertips.'[33] Eden thought *it was the high tide ... of tolerable relations between us ... the Soviet attitude would harden with the growing certainty of victory*.[34] It may be more accurate to say that Eden's own attitudes hardened, as his illusions about Soviet intentions began to dissolve.

One of the oddities of the war years was that, as Eden became more anti-Soviet, Churchill became less so. Given the latter's liking for creative tension, he may simply have decided that he should always put the opposite view to his Foreign Secretary. More likely, he thought it right to play tough with Stalin while the Russian dictator was relatively weak but to be more emollient when he became stronger. This was at least more logical than Eden's apparent policy, which uncomfortably echoed his pre-war policies: to appease weakness, but to stand firm against strength. At the first meeting of the Big Three (Churchill, Stalin and Roosevelt) in Tehran in November 1943, Eden found *the sudden shift in Stalin's policies disturbing... Above all, I began to fear greatly for the Poles*.[35] But some historians argue that Stalin's policies had scarcely changed at all and that Eden, perhaps without fully understanding it, had sold the pass on Poland and the rest of eastern Europe in Moscow the previous month.

The Russians moved into Poland early in 1944 and, despite Eden's efforts, rejected direct negotiations with the Poles on frontiers. *This was the ally for whose sake we had gone to war*, Eden recalled... . *The Polish Government and people looked to Britain for help ... but the result was beyond our reach to decide*.[36] Eden, unlike Churchill, still wanted to back the exiled Poles in London to take over in Warsaw in preference to a pro-Soviet regime. By now, the pro-Soviet Harvey had switched to another Foreign Office job, and this may partly explain Eden's change of tack. Harvey's successor, Pierson Dixon, complained in his diary that Churchill did not understand that 'plain speaking and hard bargaining produces far better results'.[37] Yet Eden never entirely lost his soft spot for Stalin. Even after Soviet forces had cynically held back from helping the anti-Nazi Warsaw Rising in 1944, which was brutally crushed, Eden minuted: *I think that Stalin comes pretty well out of the Polish record.*[38] But a sense that, in the final reckoning, he had been outsmarted by three dictators may well have influenced Eden's actions in 1956.

Stalin may well have felt that, since it took so long to get his way on the second front, he owed the British and Americans nothing. At the Tehran conference, Churchill was still trying to postpone Operation Overlord, as the planned landings in northern France were known. But Overlord went ahead in June 1944, against a background of more arguments with de Gaulle. The French leader was not even told the date of the invasion and the Americans still insisted that they, not he, would rule the country pending elections. On D-Day itself, Churchill and Eden had a huge row on the subject. *I was accused*, Eden wrote, *of trying to break up the government ... F.D.R. and he would fight the world. I didn't lose my temper and I think that I gave as good as I got.*[39] Cadogan thought it was like a girls' school in which Churchill, Roosevelt and de Gaulle behaved as if they were 'approaching the age of puberty'.[40] Only as France was liberated, and its administration fell naturally into the hands of the Resistance, which

The Polish Government and people looked to Britain for help ... but the result was beyond our reach to decide.

EDEN

acknowledged de Gaulle as its chief, was this issue – *the cause of so many hard feelings*, as Eden put it[41] – finally resolved. The Committee of National Liberation got formal recognition in October and, on 11 November 1944, Eden and Churchill marched with de Gaulle down the Champs Elysees in a symbolic re-entry to Paris. *Not for one moment did Winston stop crying*, Eden reported.[42]

But if de Gaulle became less troublesome, Churchill didn't. As the war drew to a close, normal politics revived and the Commons consumed more of Eden's time. 'We don't, for practical purposes, have a Foreign Sec. at all,' lamented Cadogan.[43] Meanwhile, Churchill, in his Minister of Defence role, had far less to do. 'As the purely military problems simplify themselves,' wrote Harvey, 'the old boy's tireless energy leads to ever closer attention to foreign affairs.'[44] Throughout the spring and summer, there was talk of Eden giving up one of his two jobs, but nothing came of it. So the arguments continued. As the two men visited Athens in the last days of 1944, in an attempt (ultimately unsuccessful) to avert a Greek civil war, Eden grumbled: *I do wish he'd let me do my own job*.[45]

Shall I go down in the history books as an appeaser?

EDEN

This was not the only respect in which the closing stages of the war had a sour taste. When Churchill and Eden flew to Moscow for a conference in October 1944, Eden was all too aware that *the Russians had already grabbed the territory they wanted*.[46] It was at this conference that Churchill produced what he called his 'naughty document' which had percentages for the interests of the great Powers in each Balkan country: for example, 'Bulgaria: Russia, 75%, The others, 25%'. Eden tried to do some bargaining with Molotov but concluded that *we must simply accept the realities of the situation, however disagreeable*. Later, he paced the rooms of the British Embassy asking: *Shall I go down in the history books as an appeaser?*[47] Even more disagreeable were the decisions to behave as if Stalin were anything other than a bloodthirsty tyrant. At an earlier stage of the war, the Germans had discovered mass graves of Polish officers at Katyn, near Smolensk. Nazi propaganda provided embellishment, but there was little doubt the Russians were responsible. So important was the wartime alliance with Stalin, however, that even the most clear-sighted supported Eden and Churchill in playing down the incident. 'We have ... used the good name of England to cover up a massacre,' concluded Owen O'Malley, British ambassador to the Polish government, but added that 'few will think that any other course would have been wise or right'.[48]

Now the Cabinet agreed to accede to a Soviet demand that Russians found in previously Nazi-controlled areas of Europe should be returned to the Soviet Union regardless of their own wishes. Eden in particular well understood that many of these men would be shot. His comments at the time – *we don't want them here* scrawled across one letter on the subject and *we cannot afford to be sentimental about this* in a minute to Churchill[49] – have been used as examples of appalling callousness. Some 40,000 anti-Communist or 'White' Russian troops, some of them in German uniform, were among those sent back to face Stalin's untender mercies and this episode would haunt Eden to the end of his life. But even his most critical biographer accepts there was no real choice, as did most anti-Soviet ministers and officials at the time. A failure to meet Stalin's demand would have unravelled agreements on post-war Europe, perhaps leaving Greece under Communist control, and endangered British prisoners-of-war who were then falling into Soviet hands. Eden can perhaps be criticised only for implementing the policy with excessive zeal.

As late as December 1944, Eden was saying that *Stalin has never broken his word once given*.[50] Some time after the Allied conference at Yalta in the southern Crimea in February 1945, involving Churchill, Roosevelt and Stalin as well as their foreign secretaries, he must surely have revised his opinion. The Yalta meetings involved tough bargaining but at the end, wrote Cadogan, 'the P.M. and Anthony are well satisfied – if not more'.[51] The Russians agreed that the French, as well as the British, Americans and Russians, should have a military control zone in post-war Germany. On Poland, by far the most important issue at Yalta, they agreed that the Communist-backed provisional government in Lublin should be reorganised 'on a broader democratic basis'. Finally, they signed a Declaration on Liberal Europe which accepted the 'right of all peoples to choose the form of government under which they will live'.

Eden found the Russians relaxed and friendly. But, he recalled, *within a few weeks all this had changed*.[52] The Russians paid no attention to Polish leaders outside Lublin and, when 16 went to Moscow to talk about all-party government, they promptly disappeared without trace. Later, it was admitted they had been arrested and some were sentenced to long terms in prison. Elsewhere in eastern Europe, it was clear the Russians were taking complete control wherever they could. *I take the gloomiest view of Russian behaviour everywhere*, Eden wrote at the end of March, ... *our foreign policy seems a sad wreck. They* [the Russians] *become more brazen by the day*, he wrote to Churchill in July.[53]

Again, charges of appeasement were circulating. But it is hard, in retrospect, to see what more could have been done.

> *Our foreign policy seems a sad wreck. They* [the Russians] *become more brazen by the day.*
>
> EDEN TO CHURCHILL

Even after the European war ended with Hitler's death and Germany's surrender in May 1945, the war with the Japanese continued and the Americans had no appetite for a new conflict in Europe. Harry Truman, who had succeeded Roosevelt as US president after the latter's death, resisted British pleas for US forces to take Prague before Stalin did. Both Churchill and Eden were now, very slowly, coming to a recognition of the realities of the post-war world. Eden had modified his anti-Americanism and now saw the need for Britain and America to combine against Soviet expansion. Churchill had modified (though not lost) his hatred for de Gaulle and saw the need for France to be the linchpin of a strong Western European bloc after the war. But neither fully understood Britain's diminished power and the impossibility of the independent foreign policy that Eden envisaged or the equal partnership with America that Churchill hoped for. In any case, they had both, as Harvey noted, become quite exhausted. 'They could no longer look at the problems properly or read the papers about them,' Harvey added.[54]

Eden's final international conference of the war at Potsdam in July 1945 was overshadowed by health, personal and political troubles. In May, he had been diagnosed with a duodenal ulcer. His troubled marriage was on the brink of a final break-up. His elder son, Simon, had been reported missing in action and his death was confirmed during the conference. And Eden, far more than Churchill, expected defeat in the general election. He had learnt both from his son and from his army contacts that *many of the fighting forces were not likely to vote for us.*[55] The election had been called almost as soon as the war in Europe was won. Because of his illness, Eden had played little part in the campaign, probably to the Tories' disadvantage. While Churchill provocatively warned that a Labour government would form a 'Gestapo',

Eden, in his solitary campaign broadcast, reassured the voters that *private enterprise and government control can and should exist side by side.* According to one observer, the whole Tory campaign hit the wrong note 'and only Eden got it right'.[56] Eden himself felt the Tories had talked down to the voters and described the campaign as *the dirtiest and cheapest* he had known.[57] Attempts to remonstrate with Churchill were met with 'you, my dear Anthony, know nothing about home affairs'. As Eden confessed to his diary, he almost harboured a wish for a Conservative defeat and dreaded the prospect of continuing as Foreign Secretary. *It is not work itself,* he wrote, *... but racket with Winston at all hours.*'[58]

The voting was over by the time Eden and Churchill went to Potsdam but, because of the delay in collecting ballot papers from the overseas forces, they had to go home in the middle of the conference for the results. To the Russians' amazement, they never returned. Labour won by a landslide and Churchill, talking alone with Eden in the Cabinet room, said: 'I shall never sit in it again. You will, but I shall not.'[59]

Chapter 6: 'I do wish the old man would go': 1945–55

So great was the 1945 landslide that, apart from Churchill and Eden, only one other Conservative member of the War Cabinet survived as an MP. There was now little chance of Churchill retiring; he wished to avenge his defeat and to show he could win an election as party leader. *He ought to resign now and write*, wrote Eden, *but he won't*.[1] For a time, there was a chance that Eden would be the first to leave frontline British politics. In 1946, he was mooted as the first United Nations Secretary General. *If this offer had been made to me, it could hardly have been refused*, he wrote later.[2] He apparently believed, as he had when the Viceroyalty of India was in the offing, that he could return to lead the Conservatives after a few years. But the offer never came.

In fact, Churchill did spend most of his time writing, appearing to make only the occasional set-piece speech. Eden was left, in effect, to lead the Opposition and, being reduced to an MP's salary, he combined this work with a number of company directorships. The two men did not make a very vigorous combination. Eden, in poor health after the strains of the war years, instinctively preferred consensus. He had worked with Labour ministers in the war, and he liked and admired them. *I am not a political warrior like Winston*, he had confided to his diary in June 1945.[3]

In any case, both he and Churchill were more comfortable with geopolitical and military issues than with domestic matters. On the former, the differences between Eden and Churchill were greater than those between Eden and his Foreign Office successor Ernest Bevin, whom Eden liked most of all the Labour ministers. Bevin frequently sought Eden's advice and, on the Labour side, the favourite jibe against him was 'hasn't Anthony Eden got fat?' By contrast, when Churchill made his famous speech at Fulton, Missouri, in 1946, declaring that 'an iron curtain has descended across the Continent', Eden was not even consulted. Eden largely disapproved, though, by 1948, he was using the phrase himself and talking once more of the dangers of appeasement.

Eden made more of a fist at opposition on the home front. But to the disgruntlement of some Conservatives, his criticisms of Labour's programme of nationalisation and social reform were muted. *It is wrong to oppose nationalisation on grounds of prejudice as it is to support nationalisation from blind subservience to a theory*, he said in 1946. In counterpoint to Labour's policy of increasing state control of industry, he revived the idea that had so attracted him in the 1920s. *Our objective is a nation-wide*

Ernest Bevin (1881–1951) was born in Somerset to poor parents, and was an orphan by the age of six. At 18 he moved to Bristol where he found work as a van driver, joining the Dockers' Union and becoming one of its paid officials before he was 30. He was the key figure in the series of union mergers which created the giant Transport and General Workers Union, whose first general secretary he became in 1921, holding the post until 1940 when he joined Churchill's wartime coalition government as Minister of Labour and National Service. In 1945 Attlee made him Foreign Secretary, a job he held until a few months before his death.

property-owning democracy, he told the 1946 party conference.[4] He envisaged not only an extension of home ownership but also profit-sharing in industry. As for the unions, *I have a strong feeling*, he wrote to Cecil, *that on our understanding of them and handling of them depend the contribution we can make to our national future.*[5] The Conservatives' Industrial Charter, published in May 1947, owed much to the atmosphere Eden had created in the party. It accepted the mixed economy and a degree of central planning and was therefore crucial in convincing voters that the Conservatives were no longer the party of unrestrained *laissez-faire*. But it was mostly the work of R A Butler and Eden's only significant role was to launch it at a rally in Wales. Churchill's support, as Butler put it, 'was not so much obtained as divined'.[6]

Churchill, as well as offering only spasmodic leadership, was showing signs of his age. He suffered a stroke in 1949. Inevitably, there were occasional bouts of intrigue against him. While privately saying *I do wish the old man would go*,[7] Eden neither encouraged nor discouraged the plotters. Yet at this time he had no serious potential rivals for the succession. Only his extra-marital affairs presented a serious threat to his future. He had some narrow escapes. Thanks to his friend Jim Thomas, the suicide of one of his lovers was covered up. The possibility that he might be cited in a divorce case came to nothing. But he took it seriously enough to warn Churchill who said, as he left the meeting, 'Anthony must be more careful in future'.[8]

The public knew nothing of these matters and Eden delayed his divorce until 1950, just long enough for social attitudes on the subject to have changed. Eden's personal popularity was undimmed, with opinion polls in 1949 suggesting the Conservatives might win more votes under his leadership. But what people liked about him was precisely what stopped him plotting against Churchill. 'Why is he one of the few men who can get a hearing from all classes?' asked the *Observer* in a profile. It was because, unlike so many politicians, he had not become 'coarsened or cunning'. This was a verdict with which Max (Lord) Beaverbrook, who had sat beside him

'He is no Mr Baldwin … Mr Baldwin was a cunning man. Mr Eden is not cunning.'

LORD BEAVERBROOK

in wartime Cabinets, would have largely agreed. 'He is no Mr Baldwin,' Beaverbrook once instructed a *Daily Express* editor. 'Mr Baldwin was a cunning man. Mr Eden is not cunning.'[9]

After an election in 1950, Labour's majority fell to a handful of seats. The government staggered on for another 18 months. Its leading ministers had been in office for more than a decade, probably the most difficult and exhausting in British history. Since 1945, they had struggled to build a welfare state in a near-bankrupt country and, in the middle of it all, had faced the worst winter of the century. They had been forced to keep rationing, which was for a period more severe than in wartime. Standard rate income tax was still nine shillings (45p) in the pound. An anti-Labour swing was probably inevitable. Even so, Labour didn't help itself by adopting a sometimes unnecessarily aggressive tone towards the middle classes. It has been well said that opposition parties don't win elections, governments lose them. In October 1951, the Conservatives were returned with a majority of 17. Yet they still got some 200,000 fewer votes than Labour. The big difference from 1950 was that the Liberal vote fell by nearly two million or 76 per cent. At least one Conservative historian has judged that, in winning over those middle-ground and mostly middle-class votes, Eden's role was crucial.

There was not much doubt that, in the new Conservative government, Eden would return to the Foreign Office. He was without rival as heir to the premiership and Churchill was expected to retire within months. Eden was not formally called deputy prime minister, but that was his position in everything but name. No Foreign Secretary in the 20th century had such undisputed autonomy and, in the view of one fellow minister, it amounted to 'an abrogation of the role of the cabinet'.[10]

Yet for the best part of four years the supreme prize would remain tantalisingly beyond his grasp. Churchill always found another reason to stay: a new monarch, following the death of George VI in 1952; a new US president, following the defeat of Harry Truman in the 1952 elections; a new regime in Russia, following Stalin's death in 1953. As the months went by, Eden became more and more exasperated. A more ruthless heir apparent, such as Harold Macmillan, would have hustled Churchill out of office within weeks. But Eden was inhibited not only by his prevaricating temperament but also by his long, affectionate association with the Prime Minister. The inhibitions grew when he married Churchill's niece, Clarissa, in August 1952 and thus became a close relative. Only in 1955, by which time his relationship with Churchill was sadly soured, did Eden finally plunge the dagger at a Cabinet meeting that Macmillan described as the most dramatic and harrowing he had known.

His relations with Churchill were made no easier by the latter's continued interference in foreign affairs and his attempts to organise personal summits with the Russian and American leaders. Eden loathed the idea of these cosy, agenda-less chats between 'the top men', particularly since they would inevitably lead to Churchill getting more of the limelight than he did. He did agree to back one of Churchill's summit plans, despite Cabinet opposition, but only in exchange for what he thought was a firm promise that, once it was over, the old man would stand aside. At times, in a petulant way, Eden would talk of retiring himself. *I get all the knocks; I don't think I can stand it much longer*, he told Channon in November 1952. In June 1954, he was saying: *I must escape somehow*.[11]

Throughout these years, the possibility that he would miss out on the premiership after all must have lurked at the back of Eden's mind. The only plausible alternative, R A Butler, was hailed as a successful Chancellor of the Exchequer and grew in political strength. In January 1953, Alan Lascelles, the Queen's private secretary, told Evelyn Shuckburgh, Eden's private secretary at the Foreign Office, that Butler might be running neck-and-neck by the end of the year. Eden became inordinately jealous of his rival: after an article in the *Sunday Times*, his wife wrote a 'ferocious letter' to Shuckburgh complaining that Butler was getting a better press and that 'everybody round Anthony ... ought to pull their socks up'.[12]

By a quirk of fate, Butler might at one point have snatched the prize. Eden, as Shuckburgh put it, was 'constantly having trouble with his insides'. His staff had to carry round 'a black tin box containing various forms of analgesic ... ranging from simple aspirins to morphia injections ... These pains ... undoubtedly coloured his judgment. For one thing, they deprived him of sleep.'[13] In April 1953, Eden's doctors concluded that this chronic ill-health was caused by gallstones and an operation was necessary. Unfortunately, the senior surgeon was reduced almost to a nervous wreck by Churchill's constant messages (which continued to the moment the anaesthetic was administered) reiterating the eminence of the patient and the national importance of a successful outcome.

I get all the knocks; I don't think I can stand it much longer.

EDEN

As Eden put it, *the knife slipped*. A vital organ was cut and it was left to the junior surgeon – who kept repeating 'blood, blood, I have never seen so much blood' – to clear up the mess. The junior carried out a second operation, during which Eden nearly died. Eden had to be taken to America – much to Churchill's chagrin, because he feared it would reflect badly on British medicine – for a third operation, using the latest medical procedures and lasting eight hours.

The situation became still more complicated when, in June, Churchill had another stroke – an event that, with the co-operation of the newspaper proprietors, was hushed up. He was not as badly affected as first feared. But had Eden been in action, he would almost certainly have been persuaded to retire. Equally, if the stroke had made Churchill unable or unwilling to continue working, the pressure would have been on the sick Eden to stand aside, even though there were plans for Lord Salisbury (formerly Cranborne, formerly Cecil) to head an interim government. Butler would then, in all probability, have succeeded.

As it was, both Churchill and Eden continued. Considering the doctors' prognosis before the third operation – that his chances of surviving at all were only 50–50, and his chances of leading an active life barely one in ten – the latter made a remarkable recovery and what many considered the finest and most productive year of his political life was still to come. Nevertheless, he was left, as he later put it, *with a largely artificial inside*[14] and could keep going only with the aid of drugs and stimulants.

Ill-health and frustration bordering on anger with Churchill were thus the backdrop to Eden's third spell as Foreign Secretary. The most urgent problem on his desk in 1951 was Iran and the threat that developments there posed to Britain's oil interests. The Iranian prime minister,

Mohammed Mossadeq ('Mussy Duck', Churchill called him), had nationalised the Anglo-Iranian Oil Company. The Labour government had sent troops to the area. The Americans, however, opposed military action. The British view, to which Eden subscribed, was that Mossadeq, if dealt with firmly, might mend his ways or be replaced by someone better. The American view was that he might be replaced by Communists. One country wished to overthrow Mossadeq, with boycotts and the like; the other wished to keep him in power, with economic and even military aid.

This difference brought Eden into the first of the conflicts with the Americans that were to dominate the rest of his political life. In his memoirs, Eden suggested that the differences with Dean Acheson, US Secretary of State (equivalent of Foreign Secretary) under Truman, were amicable and that the real problems – which were to become most acute during the Suez crisis of 1956 – began when John Foster Dulles took over under the Republican President Dwight Eisenhower. In fact, Eden and Acheson exchanged harsh words about Iran on several occasions. In taped recollections in 1954, the latter was scathing (to some extent unfairly) about Eden's stubbornness and arrogance: 'he knew the Persians; he had been there and in his view they were rug dealers and that's all they were.'[15]

The truth was that Eden struggled to come to terms with Britain's changed relationship with the Americans in the 1950s. The British were now heavily in debt to their transatlantic allies; if the Empire were to survive at all, it would do so on American sufferance. Eden recognised America's superior resources and tried to engage her as a partner in, for example, the Middle East. He did not recognise the extent to which the Americans could now determine the rules of the game; that, as one of Dulles's biographers put it, 'a Dulles monosyllable (or even his silence) could mean more than Eden's most eloquent peroration'.[16] His aim, he explained to the Cabinet in 1953, was *to persuade the United States to assume the real burdens ... while retaining for ourselves as much political control – and hence prestige and world influence – as we can.*[17] He completely misjudged the extent to which the Americans would tolerate this role as a sort of British gofer. They wanted to be leaders, not partners. Because Dulles sabotaged him at Suez in 1956, and thus ended his political career, Eden chose to personalise this clash. In his diary, Eden described Dulles as *a meanly jealous man* whose *diplomatic moves were as tortuous as a wounded snake's.*[18] But on Mossadeq, Eden eventually eased Dulles and the Republican administration round to his view and a joint British-US secret service operation – which Eden, perhaps understandably, failed to mention in his memoirs – brought down the Iranian premier in 1954.

Eden, like many Englishmen of his generation, saw the Americans as vulgar, boastful upstarts, and this view had been accentuated during the war. They had, he wrote in January 1944, *a much exaggerated conception of the military contribution they are making.* After a visit to Washington in 1952, he recorded that, though the Americans were polite and listen to what we have to say, they *make (on most issues) their own decisions.*[19] Eden professed horror at this behaviour. For their part, US politicians and officials found it hard to deal with a man who addressed members of his own sex as *my dear* and seemed, as a member of Dulles's staff put it, to carry a 'rather calculatedly lazy manner, which is one of the upper-class manifestations of the old English aristocracy'.[20] When the Republicans took office, these mutual suspicions were rein-

... a meanly jealous man {whose} diplomatic moves were as tortuous as a wounded snake's.

EDEN ON DULLES

forced by Dulles's tactile manner and notorious halitosis. In Eden's mind, it probably didn't help that Churchill, himself half-American, seemed to strike more of a chord with the American governing class.

Eden was above all an Empire and Commonwealth man. *For us, Empire must always come first*, he wrote in 1949.[21] He was, as one of his biographers put it, 'the last of the Liberal Imperialists'.[22] If he wanted to assert independence from the Americans, he was equally anxious to protect Britain from any surrender of sovereignty to Europe. It is perhaps unfair to call him the first Eurosceptic, since his views were almost universally shared in Britain at the time and only Macmillan and a few others showed enthusiasm for closer British involvement.

But on Europe his views were uncharacteristically blunt. Much of his anti-European reputation rests on his categorical statement in 1951 that Britain would play no part in either the Pleven Plan for a European Army (which came to nothing) or the Schuman Plan for a European Coal and Steel Community (which would lead to today's European Union). Eden's words were seen then as a repudiation of more pro-Europe remarks made by David Maxwell Fyfe, the Home Secretary, a few days earlier. They were greeted as a betrayal

John Foster Dulles (1888–1959) served as Secretary of State under President Eisenhower from 1953 to 1959. Staunchly anti-communist, he was instrumental in building up NATO and forming its sister organisation the Southeast Asia Treaty Organisation in 1954. He advocated a policy of 'liberation' rather than 'containment' of perceived Communist expansion and backed US support for the French in Indo-China. Despite opposing Eden over Suez, by 1958 he prevented the US supplying arms to Nasser, which may have driven him into the Soviet camp. He died of cancer in 1959.

by British pro-Europeans and by many on the Continent. In fact, the difference was only one of tone. The substance of what the two men said was almost identical and it represented Cabinet policy.

That policy was to encourage European unity which, as Eden well understood, ultimately meant a federal Europe, with loss of sovereignty for its member nations. *We want a united Europe*, he wrote to Churchill in 1951. *There is no doubt about that*.[23] But as he said in a lecture in America in January 1952, joining such a federation *is something which we know, in our bones, we cannot do*. Without its *family ties* in the Commonwealth, Britain would be *no more than some millions of people living on an island off the coast of Europe, in which nobody wants to take any particular interest*.[24]

If Eden now seems misguided on this subject, it has to be acknowledged that Britain in the early 1950s could still play a significantly autonomous role on the world stage. This was most evident at the Geneva conference of 1954, which brought peace (albeit temporarily) to Indo-China and was described by one historian as 'Britain's swan song as a Great Power'.[25] The stated purpose of the conference – which initially involved the British, French, Americans, Chinese and Russians – was to bring about the reunification of Korea, divided as a result of a recent truce in the Korean War. It ended with the division of another Asian country. Yet such was the mood of the times that this was regarded as a triumph.

Eden described Indo-China as *the most dangerous and acute of the problems with which I had to deal during my last four years as Foreign Secretary*. The French empire in south-east Asia was in meltdown. In Vietnam, the main focus of nationalist feeling was with Ho Chi Minh's Vietminh forces, which were supported by the Chinese Communists. The Americans were not directly involved, but were meeting nearly half the costs of the French war effort. They feared that, if the rebels won, Malaya, Burma and Indonesia, and the neighbouring French colonies Cambodia and Laos, would also go Communist. They drew comparisons with the Japanese invasion of Manchuria in 1931 and Hitler's reoccupation of the Rhineland in 1936. *I was not convinced*, recalled Eden.[26] He feared, as did many others, that the Americans would provoke a Third World War.

These fears became all the greater on the eve of the Geneva Conference. First, Dulles came to London, arguing that China should be threatened with military action if she didn't stop aiding the Vietminh. This action, he argued, should be shared by a coalition including Britain. Dulles left London believing that Eden had agreed to the coalition's urgent formation. But in Eden's view – the difference was probably a genuine misunderstanding – he had agreed only to a long-term fallback if Geneva failed. *I was determined*, he recalled, *that we would not be hustled into injudicious military decisions.*[27] When Dulles, back in Washington, called meetings to set up the coalition, Eden instructed the British Ambassador not to attend. In the Commons he made the limits of what he thought he had agreed quite clear. Dulles felt badly let down. 'Eden has double-crossed me,' he wrote to his sister. 'He lied to me.'[28]

Then at a NATO meeting in Paris, word came that an important French base at Dien Bien Phu was about to fall. US air strikes, the French said, were needed within 72 hours. The Americans were ready to agree but needed British support in order to get Congressional approval. Eden, fearing British action would split the Commonwealth, refused. *I told Mr Dulles that he was confronting British opinion with about as difficult a decision as it would be possible to find.*[29]

As the Geneva conference opened, Eden's mood, noted Shuckburgh, was virulently anti-American. He and Dulles 'have got thoroughly on each other's nerves, and are both behaving rather like prima donnas'. The Americans, complained Eden, *want to run the world*.[30] Within a week, Dulles had stormed out of the conference. *The trouble with you, Foster*, said Eden as he left, *is that you want World War Three*.[31] Dulles left his deputy behind to represent US interests and he proved more co-operative with Eden's ambitions for a settlement. However, the Americans remained, as Eden put it, *deeply apprehensive of reaching any agreement, however innocuous, with the Communists*.[32] Increasingly, he found himself allied with Molotov, the Soviet foreign minister, in trying to cajole their reluctant allies — the Americans and Chinese respectively — into an agreement. Eden saw nothing wrong with this. The hydrogen bomb already existed, but intercontinental ballistic missiles that could hit the US or China didn't. *It is the two countries likely to suffer most from bombing ... that are most anxious to work out a settlement*, argued Eden.[33]

> *The trouble with you, Foster, is that you want World War Three.*
>
> EDEN TO DULLES

The conference was, as Eden put it, *a long and wearisome business*,[34] lasting nearly three months, albeit with interruptions. The final agreement included the partition of an independent Vietnam between a communist north and a non-communist south and the promise (never realised) of free elections. To Eden's indignation, the Americans refused to guarantee it, since they would not recognise a Communist regime. They merely promised not to disturb the settlement. The conference was widely hailed as a diplomatic triumph for Eden. But it did little for Anglo-American relations. According to the British Ambassador in Washington, Dulles had been 'deeply wounded' when 'the American press cheerfully recorded that he had suffered the worst defeat in American diplomatic history' while Eden was being showered with bouquets.[35] And once more, there was the whiff of appeasement. *Punch* ran a cartoon of Eden returning from Geneva dressed like Chamberlain, complete with an umbrella.

Indo-China was not Eden's only success in 1954, a year that was to see him win an international peace prize, the accolade 'politician of the year' from the *Daily Mirror*, and the Order of the Garter (making him Sir Anthony Eden) from the Queen. At Geneva, he secured a peace that would last only a few years. With hindsight, therefore, another achievement – a Western European settlement that would last for 35 years, until the fall of the Berlin Wall – was more impressive.

By 1954, it was clear that the French were too suspicious of the Germans to join a European Defence Community (EDC). But something had to be done. The Americans wouldn't continue to bear the main burden of defending West Germany against Communist encroachment. The Germans had to play some role in protecting themselves, but nobody wanted a new German army that might go its own way. The answer – which Eden claimed to have hit upon in his bath – was to bring the Germans into NATO. The French were still reluctant to agree. So were the Americans. They hoped eventually for a United States of Europe, and Eden's proposal, unlike the EDC, didn't bring that any closer. Eden pulled another rabbit from the hat. Britain would join a Western European Union, which would co-ordinate the region's independent armies, and promised to keep a permanent military presence on the Continent. This, wrote Eden, was *a very formidable step for us to take*,[36] because Britain was historically averse to stationing troops across the Channel. But it did the trick with the French and the Americans. It also made Eden even more of a certainty for the premiership. But as the prize came within his grasp, his nemesis was already looming. Egypt had been Eden's most persistent and troublesome problem since his return to office. On this, his differences with Churchill were most acute and his behaviour over Suez is 1956 is impossible to understand without a grasp of the political difficulties that Egypt caused him in the preceding years.

The story of Eden and Egypt, indeed, goes right back to his first spell as Foreign Secretary. Though never technically a colony, Egypt had been virtually under British administration since 1882 and formally became a protectorate early in the First World War. Nationalist feeling was strong but attempts to negotiate independence always foundered on British insistence on her rights to defend the Suez Canal. Eden had untied this knot in 1936. The British would withdraw, but would keep a specified number of troops on Egyptian soil, mainly to protect the canal, whose international character Egypt agreed to recognise.

The 1936 treaty was due for renewal in 1956 but, against the rising tide of Arab nationalism, the prospects seemed poor. As Shuckburgh, who served in Egypt before he worked for Eden, noted, it 'was still regarded as outlying territory of the Raj'.[37] The British Ambassador drove through Cairo with motorcyclists blowing whistles before him and behaved more like a colonial governor than a diplomatic representative. In 1952, the country exploded into violence. British troops killed 43 Egyptians at Ismalia in a punitive response to the sabotage of their water supplies. Riots followed in Cairo, with nine British subjects killed and the Shepheard's Hotel, a symbol of the British presence, set on fire. Eden wished the Suez Canal to remain under British control, since he saw it as a vital lifeline for the Empire. He was not so keen to keep the military base. *The tangled mass of workshops and railways in an area the size of Wales*, he recalled, *was cumbersome and dependent upon Egyptian labour ... Smaller bases, redeployment and dispersal would serve our purposes better.*

In July 1952, a military regime, in which Colonel Gamal Abdul Nasser was prominent, took over in Egypt. The regime *showed no signs as yet of those wider ambitions of empire which Colonel Nasser was later to proclaim and pursue*[38] and Eden began talks. Tory backbenchers sniffed a sell-out and formed a Suez Group to support the continuation of the military base. Churchill's sympathy for the backbenchers' views was clear. Returning from holidays in Jamaica in January 1953, Shuckburgh heard that he 'was in a rage against A.E., speaking of "appeasement" and saying that he never knew before that Munich was situated on the Nile'. Eden recalled: *I should have had to resign if I had not got my way*. Churchill was reported to have said: 'If he resigns, I shall accept it and take the Foreign Office myself.'[39] Churchill was eventually coaxed into agreeing that negotiations could continue on the canal. In Shuckburgh's words, he dropped 'his idea that we could not possibly go until a lot of people had been killed'.[40]

But he continued to snipe at Eden's policy, making it all the more difficult to pacify the backbenchers. It was, he said in Cabinet meetings, 'an igno-

'What security have we got that the Egyptians ... will keep any agreement that you will make with them?'

CHURCHILL TO EDEN

minious surrender of our responsibilities'.[41] 'What security have we got,' Churchill asked Eden, in words that no doubt resonated in the latter's ears in 1956, 'that the Egyptians ... will keep any agreement that you will make with them?'.[42] At one stage, Eden wrote out a resignation letter, though Shuckburgh thought it just 'a pure manoeuvre which he had no intention of pressing'.[43] The Americans, Eden felt, were of little help on this subject. They saw Arab nationalism as the best defence against Communism. They appeared, Eden recalled, to want *a quick solution at almost any cost* and withheld *the wholehearted support which their partner in N.A.T.O. had the right to expect.*[44]

By March 1954, following a warning from the Chief Whip, even Eden got cold feet. 'He is beginning to find the unpopularity of his Egyptian policy in his party too heavy a burden,' wrote Shuckburgh, 'and is seeking ways of abandoning it.'[45] He toyed with the idea of delaying a final agreement until Churchill had retired. But since Churchill showed few signs of stepping down, Eden had to press ahead. An agreement was signed later that year. Britain would evacuate her troops within 20 months, but British civilians would maintain the canal base for a further seven years and the Suez Canal Company would continue to run it. Egypt declared its support for international freedom of navigation through the canal and accepted that Britain could re-enter the zone in an emergency.

Though the Egyptian canker had apparently been removed, Eden's relations with Churchill didn't improve. Their fragility was demonstrated to Selwyn Lloyd, a junior minister at the FO, when Churchill wanted to make a Commons statement on the progress of the Geneva conference. When Eden spoke to him on the phone from Geneva, 'the line nearly fused', recalled Lloyd. Afterwards, Churchill 'stalked up and down the room saying A was the most selfish man he had ever known, thought only of himself, had to do everything himself, was a prima donna, and quite impossible to work with'.[46]

The pressure on Churchill grew, with ministers complaining, as Eden put it, *about drawling Cabinets, the failure to take decisions* and Eden himself slowly coming more into the open. *The old man feels bitterly towards me, but this I cannot help*, wrote Eden.[47] Churchill, now past his 80th birthday, agreed to go at Easter 1955 but when, in February that year, a new Russian

leadership took over, under Bulganin and Khrushchev, he saw another chance for his precious summit. Moreover, he envisaged joining Eisenhower in Paris for the tenth anniversary of VE-Day.

In mid-March, Eden had to force the issue, saying in a Cabinet meeting: *I have been Foreign Secretary for 10 years. Am I not to be trusted?*[48] 'The ensuing days,' wrote Colville, Churchill's private secretary, 'were painful. W. began to form a cold hatred of Eden who, he repeatedly said, had done more to thwart him and prevent him pursuing the policy he thought right than anybody else.'[49] To the end, Churchill talked of staying on. On 1 April, he told his doctor: 'I don't want to go, but Anthony wants it so much.'[50] Three days later, after a farewell dinner with 50 guests, including the Queen and Prince Philip, he spent his last night in Downing Street. He sat on his bed, wearing his Garter, Order of Merit and knee-breeches, and said: 'I don't believe Anthony can do it.'[51]

Part Two

THE LEADERSHIP

Chapter 7: Suez: 1955–6

By the end of 1955, many people shared Churchill's view. In his first months as Prime Minister, Eden acquired a reputation for dither, weakness and fussiness. His popularity, in Noel Coward's words, 'sputtered away like a bob of fat in a frying pan'.[1] Yet in May, Eden comfortably won a general election, becoming the first incumbent Prime Minister since Palmerston to increase his party's majority and winning, albeit on a reduced turnout, 49.4 per cent of the vote, the fourth highest share of the 20th century. Eden's trustworthy personality and reputation as a man of peace were central to the campaign. In the first election where TV played a role, he spoke, he recalled, *direct to the British people for 15 minutes without company and without script.*[2]

Eden, however, 'never built a Cabinet in his own mould', as one of his ministers put it.[3] He did not, as expected, reshuffle the government on taking office, even though people had been grumbling for years about too many old men being in control. To greater surprise, no reshuffle followed the election. The changes came just before Christmas. They were still relatively modest: the Home and Colonial Offices, the Board of Trade, the Ministries of Agriculture, Education and War were among the departments where the man at the top was unchanged. But Harold Macmillan went from the Foreign Office to the Treasury, replacing R A Butler who became

Leader of the Commons. Neither was pleased. Macmillan had been at the FO for only six months, and Butler felt he had been demoted. The latter was told that he was, in effect, deputy prime minister; the former was told this wasn't true.

Eden's failure to freshen up the government can plausibly be blamed on his lifetime in the FO. He simply did not know enough Tory MPs well enough to know which were worth promoting. Backbenchers and junior ministers, many of whom found Eden an aloof and distant figure, were naturally frustrated. Unrest among ministers was accentuated by what Butler called 'his conscientious but highly strung supervision of our affairs'.[4] He would ring ministers at all hours, to ask what they were doing about some minor problem, and often flew into a temper if not satisfied with their answers. He insisted, for example, on checking appointments to the boards of nationalised industries with the result, as one minister recalled, 'that they were then held up in his office for embarrassingly long periods'.[5] He did to his Foreign Secretaries precisely what he had complained that Chamberlain and Churchill did to him, even trying to arrange personal summits with the Russians. 'I might as well give up and let him run the shop,' grumbled Macmillan.[6] According to one account, Selwyn Lloyd, who succeeded Macmillan at the FO, was rung 30 times during his first weekend in the job.

'I might as well give up and let him {Eden} run the shop'

MACMILLAN

The economic situation added to the government's troubles. After several years of steady improvement, Britain faced a sterling crisis and rising inflation. Butler, after a tax-cutting pre-election budget, introduced a new package in October clawing back twice as much as he had previously disbursed. It didn't help when Butler told a posh dinner: 'We must not drop back into easy evenings with port wine and over-ripe pheasant.'[7] Labour elected a new leader, Hugh Gaitskell, in December. He seemed younger, fresher and, on domestic issues, more confident than Eden.

The press began to turn on Eden and his government. Clarissa Eden was pilloried when she asked a tenant on the Chequers estate to refrain from putting her washing on the line in full view of the house. When the *Daily Telegraph* ran an article calling for 'the smack of firm government', Anthony Nutting, an Eden protege who was now Minister of State at the FO, 'had never seen Eden so stricken'.[8] The feeling that he could not be a strong leader in the Churchill mould was exactly what worried Eden most. By January 1956, he was being forced to deny he would resign in the summer. Butler, leaving London Airport on holiday, was reported to have said Eden was 'the best Prime Minister we have got', though all he had actually said was 'yes' to a journalist's question.

Always sensitive to press criticism, Eden insisted on attacking *cantankerous newspapers* in a speech in Bradford. Later that month, Shuckburgh, accompanying him on a journey to Washington, wrote: 'I don't think he is at all well or happy.' Later in the trip, he added: 'He has ... changed greatly in the last two years. He is far away, thinking largely about the effect he is making, not in any way strengthened in character ... by the attainment of his ambition.'[9] Macmillan may have sensed Eden's growing weakness when he threatened to resign in February. The Chancellor wished to abolish bread and milk subsidies; Eden didn't. After seven Cabinet meetings, Eden conceded that the milk subsidy should go immediately and the bread subsidy be phased out.

This was the background to the events in Egypt that would dominate Eden's premiership and ultimately snatch from him the prize for which he had waited so long. By now, Nasser had emerged as Egypt's undisputed ruler. The fear that he would throw in his lot with the Soviets was growing. In September 1955, he announced a deal to buy Soviet arms through Czechoslovakia. Western leaders, particularly Eden, feared that Russia would increase further its influence by financing Nasser's grand project, the Aswan High Dam. *If the Russians get the contract*, Eden told the Americans in January 1956, *we have lost Africa*.[10] Eden was at this stage apparently still in favour of wooing Nasser over to the West, though on the January visit to America, he had told Shuckburgh that the man was *a cad* and compared him to Mussolini. When Shuckburgh demurred, 'he all but called me an appeaser'.[11]

Now came the first chapter – and, in some accounts, a decisive one – in the drama that was to lead to Eden's fall. On 1 March, King Hussein of Jordan dismissed General Sir John Glubb, the British-born commander of his armed forces. Jordan, until recently under British administration, was still a heavily-subsidised British client state. Its armed forces, known as the Arab Legion, were led by British officers. It was central to British strategy for the Middle East, which involved strengthening the Baghdad Pact, an alliance of Britain, Iraq, Turkey, Pakistan, Iran and eventually, Eden hoped, Jordan. The young Hussein may have been the ruler of an independent country, but he had no excuse, in Eden's

Gamal Adel Nasser (1918–70) was one of the army officers who staged a coup in Egypt in 1952. Becoming President in 1956, his defiance of the former colonial powers over the Suez Canal won him widespread popularity in the Arab world. In 1958 he formed the United Arab Republic with Syria, but this collapsed three years later. Defeat by Israel in the Six-Day War of 1967 was a major blow, leading to his temporary resignation. He died of a heart attack in 1970. (See *Life&Times: Nasser* by Anne Alexander.)

view, for dismissing a British soldier *like a pilfering servant*.[12] Furthermore Eden blamed Nasser, whose anti-British propaganda was now intense, for Glubb's fate. Further evidence of his malign influence came from Bahrain, where the visiting Selwyn Lloyd was stoned.

To many Tory backbenchers, Eden was the man who had tried to appease Nasser by evacuating the Suez Canal zone. Now, as Eden feared and expected, they wanted his blood. Julian Amery, a leader of the Suez Group, wrote to the *Times* declaring the 'bankruptcy of a policy of appeasement in the Middle East'. 'The events in Jordan,' wrote Clarissa Eden in her diary, 'have shattered A.'[13] When MPs debated Jordan, Eden lost his temper and, on his own estimation, made the worst Commons speech of his life. *My friends were embarrassed and my critics exultant*, he recalled.[14]

Eden cooled down on King Hussein – he did not, for example, stop British aid – but Nasser was a different matter. According to Shuckburgh, he was 'quite emphatic that Nasser must be got rid of' and said: *It's either him or us, don't forget it.*[15] Nutting claimed to have spent half the night arguing with Eden after Glubb's dismissal.

'On that fatal day,' Nutting wrote, 'he decided that the world was not big enough to hold both him and Nasser.' Later, when Nutting produced a routine FO memorandum about future relations with Egypt, Eden exploded: *What's all this nonsense about isolating Nasser … I want him destroyed, can't you understand?*[16]

> *What's all this nonsense about isolating Nasser … I want him destroyed, can't you understand?*
>
> EDEN

Nutting claimed that the Suez débâcle, or something similar, was inevitable from this moment. That is probably an exaggeration. But Eden's foreign policy now entered a harder phase. For example, in Cyprus, a British colony pressing for independence, the leader of the Greek community, Archbishop Makarios, was accused of involvement with Eoka, a terrorist group. Instead of simply being deported, as the Colonial Office proposed, Makarios was incarcerated on a remote island in the Seychelles. Eden, recalled Nutting, had 'decided that the time had come for the British lion not only to roar at its adversary, but to gobble him up altogether'.[17] The Tory criticism died away. One Tory MP, Nigel Nicolson, recalled that his constituents 'cheered themselves hoarse' at the news of Makarios's arrest and 'it was really from this moment onwards that he [Eden] felt his role to be that of the strong man'.[18] Perhaps after all he could emerge from Churchill's shadow. Eden now turned against financing Nasser's dam. The Americans finally pulled the plug on the project after Egypt had recognised Communist China. Days later, on 26 July, Nasser announced the nationalisation of the Suez Canal Company, arguing that he needed the revenues to finance Aswan. It was, wrote Eden, *an event which changed all perspectives*.[19]

Even after 50 years, many details of what happened over the next four months remain murky. Some documents are still secret, others were destroyed. Few participants would ever speak frankly about the events, and fewer would do so for direct quotation. Dates are disputed, memoirs are unreliable and it is alleged that even the visitors' book at Chequers was falsified. The voluminous literature includes vivid accounts of meetings and of who said what; but some of those quoted denied they were present, or even that particular meetings took place at all. Alongside Munich, Suez divided the British more deeply than any event of the 20th century. In some ways, the divisions (though they would be more quickly healed) were at the time more bitter, because troops, then including conscripts, were in action. The divisions cut across political parties, families and friendships and, as one of Eden's biographers recalled, 'dinner parties became hazardous'.[20]

The Suez Canal was imprinted on British minds as the Empire's most precious asset. It was the essential line of supply to and from Australia, New Zealand, India and other Asian countries. Though many of these had now achieved independence, nearly all had joined the Commonwealth, which Britain still saw as a source of strength. It was largely to protect the canal that Britain had been drawn into the Middle East in the first place and into a military occupation of Egypt that had only just ended. The canal was the conduit for three-quarters of Western Europe's oil and it was widely believed, as the *Times* put it, that Egypt, 'a nation of... low technical and managerial skills', wouldn't be able to manage it.

The Americans depended on the canal to a far lesser extent. Their chief concerns in the Middle East were to contain Soviet Russia and to bring about Arab-Israeli peace. They thought Arab nationalism might be a bulwark against Communism and that Nasser, precisely because he was strong, might be able to settle with Israel. As Foreign Secretary, Eden failed to develop a policy that took sufficient account of these differences. It may be objected that, when the Americans equated nationalism and communism in the Far East, it was perverse of them not to do so in the Middle East. But that does not excuse Eden who, as we have seen, never quite grasped that the onus was now on Britain to adjust her policies to American foibles, not the other way round.

Since Britain and the US, whatever the latter's anti-colonialist rhetoric, both regarded non-white countries as existing only for the West's convenience, their differences over Nasser and other Middle Eastern issues often seemed ones of mere detail and emphasis. Almost throughout the Suez crisis, Eden and other British ministers compared the increasingly heated arguments between London and Washington to a family tiff. 'Not having the Americans on the same side, or at least benevolently neutral,' wrote Lloyd, 'was unthinkable.'[21] It was a fatal misjudgement. The small differences widened to a chasm.

Eden first heard of Nasser's action during a dinner at Downing Street with the King and senior ministers of Iraq, another British client state. Their advice was 'hit him hard, hit him soon, and hit him by yourself'.[22] That was also the mood of the country in the following days. All seemed to agree that Nasser could not be allowed, in Eden's words, *to have his thumb on our windpipe*.[23] In the Commons, Gaitskell was at least as bellicose as Eden. Even the Foreign Office, despite its pro-Arab reputation, seemed to agree that Nasser was a mortal threat; its permanent secretary Ivone Kirkpatrick predicted, within two years, 'our standard of living reduced to that of the Yugoslavs or Egyptians'.[24] The left-wing press vied with the Tory papers in patriotic fervour: 'No More Hitlers' urged the *Daily Herald*. Across the Channel, Britain's French allies were even more outraged. They saw Nasser as a subversive influence in their rebellious North African colony of Algeria.

All the first pressures on Eden, therefore, were to follow the Iraqis' advice. Had he been able to do so – and mounted 'a straight bash' as some called it – he might have got away with it. But at a midnight meeting after the canal seizure, the chiefs of staff explained that, for all practical purposes, a military operation would take several weeks to prepare. The last British troops had left the Canal Zone a few weeks earlier in accordance with the 1954 agreement that Eden had negotiated. Malta, the nearest appropriate base to launch a seaborne invasion, was a thousand miles away. As William Clark, Eden's press adviser, recalled: 'It was suddenly obvious that Britain was armed to participate in a nuclear armageddon with the Soviet Union or in small colonial guerrilla wars … but had no capacity for this kind of emergency.'[25]

Even so, the Cabinet was clear that if Nasser didn't quickly back down military action would follow. Its Egypt Committee, formed as soon as the crisis began, talked of an 'immediate' goal of 'bringing about the downfall of the present Egyptian government'.[26] The view that 'regime change', to use the term in common currency nearly half-a-century later, was at this stage the primary British aim is supported by a decision on 10 August to change the invasion plans. The forces would land at Alexandria, within marching distance of Cairo, not at Port Said, closer to the Canal Zone.

Yet it was far from clear that Nasser's action was any more illegal than, say, British Labour's nationalisation of the railways. The canal company was technically an Egyptian company and Nasser had offered full compensation to the foreign shareholders. The law officers later discovered a few flimsy legal fig leaves for the proposed British action, but these were really beside the point. *We should not allow ourselves to become involved in legal quibbles*, wrote Eden to President Eisenhower … *we are unlikely to attain our objective by economic pressures alone … My colleagues and I are convinced that we must be ready, in the last resort, to use force to bring Nasser to his senses*. Later, he wrote that *the parallel with Mussolini is close … The removal of Nasser and the installation in Egypt of a regime less hostile to the West must therefore … rank high among our objectives*.[27] The more pro-Eden historians have made much of 'the last resort' in the first letter. But the overall tone would have made Eisenhower wonder what other resorts there could possibly be.

Eisenhower was alarmed, particularly when he learnt that Macmillan (in defiance of the military realities) had told an American minister over dinner in London that action could start in August. Macmillan's diaries (which are probably to be trusted as little as anything else Macmillan said or wrote)

> 'We must keep the Americans really frightened, ... Then they will help us to get what we want without the use of force.'
>
> HAROLD MACMILLAN

suggest this was deliberate and it had Eden's approval. 'We must keep the Americans really frightened,' he wrote. '... Then they will help us to get what we want without the use of force.'[28]

Eisenhower ordered Dulles to fly immediately to London with a personal letter to Eden. This could hardly have been blunter. Military force should not even be contemplated without prior attempts to find a peaceful solution, Eisenhower wrote. 'Public opinion here, and I am convinced in most of the world, would be outraged should there be a failure to make such efforts.'[29] But Dulles himself was less emphatic. Indeed, he said that 'a way had to be found to make Nasser disgorge what he was attempting to swallow', words which, Eden later claimed, *rang in my ears for months*.[30] If so, Eden was hearing what he wanted to hear. It is true that, throughout the crisis, Dulles blew hot and cold on the British and that he, too, hated Nasser. But Eisenhower was wedded to the romantic view that, as the first nation to shake off British colonial oppression, the US was the natural leader of newly independent nations. Eden misjudged the extent to which he would prevail over Dulles. In particular, he underestimated the importance of the forthcoming presidential campaign in which Eisenhower would seek re-election as a man of peace. Though Eisenhower counselled delay, and never ruled out military action, the closer he got to the November elections, the less likely he was to support it. To send British troops into the front line the day before Americans went to the polls, as Eden eventually did, was an act of extraordinary bad timing.

'Special Relationship'

'At this point, the United States saved Nasser. Although the administration had pressured Britain to sign the Anglo-Egyptian treaty by which all British troops had been removed from Suez and had withdrawn the Aswan Dam offer, thus precipitating Nasser's seizure of the canal and the British attack, it now opposed the use of force to settle this issue.

The reason was that [the US] saw his foreign policy in terms of a reaction against Israel and Western colonialism. If Israel had not existed, and if Egypt and the Arab states had not long been subjected and exploited by the Western powers (especially Britain), Arab nationalism would not be anti-Western and pro-Soviet. The administration therefore saw the invasion of Egypt as a golden opportunity to win Egyptian and Arab friendship. When the Jews had originally proclaimed the state of Israel, the United States had, because of domestic political considerations, recognized the new state within eleven minutes. Here was a chance to show the Arabs that the United States was not as pro-Jewish as they thought it to be, and that the country could even be pro-Arab. Since Egypt's actions were also the product of its anti-British resentment, it would be beneficial to oppose the British attempt to reassert control over the Suez Canal. By saving Nasser, the United States could align itself with Arab nationalism; supporting Britain, France, and Israel would have left the Soviet Union as the sole champion of Arab aspirations. American opposition to the invasion would, in short, identify the United States with the anti-colonialism of the entire underdeveloped world, and particularly with the anti-Israeli and nationalistic sentiments of the Arab world. Since continued evidence of British power in the Middle East only antagonized the Arabs, the destruction of this power and its replacement by American influence would be in the interest not only of the United States, but of all the Western powers. In this way, the West's strategic and economic interest could be more adequately safeguarded.' (Spanier, John: *American Foreign Policy Since World War II* (9th edition, Holt, Rinehart and Winston, New York: 1983) p 91)

In August, however, with no chance of military action for at least a month, Eden had nothing to lose by talking and considering peaceful solutions. First, he agreed to a conference of 22 maritime nations, held in London. This decided to ask Nasser if he would agree to an international body supervising the canal in association with the UN. Second, he supported a fall-back proposal from Dulles to form a Suez Canal Users' Association which would employ pilots, collect dues and pay 'a fair share' to Egypt. Eden thought it was *a cockeyed idea but if it means the Americans are with us then I think we can accept it*.[31]

With Nasser showing little enthusiasm for either idea, Eden's views seemed to harden. For example, on 6 September – replying to an even more categorical warning from Eisenhower that 'American public opinion flatly rejects the thought of using force' and that he doubted he could give even non-military support – Eden wrote: *We have many times led Europe in the fight for freedom. It would be an ignoble end to our long history if we tamely accepted to perish by degrees*.[32] Yet having agreed to try the various peaceful options proposed, Eden could not easily start a war without exhausting them.

We have many times led Europe in the fight for freedom. It would be an ignoble end to our long history if we tamely accepted to perish by degrees.

EDEN

American opposition was becoming daily more apparent. The US had not even ordered all its ships to withhold canal dues from the Egyptians, nor entirely frozen Egyptian dollar holdings as Britain had frozen sterling holdings. To Eden's fury, Dulles told a press conference that, if Nasser rejected the users' association, 'we do not intend to shoot our way through'. In effect, Eden argued in his memoirs, Dulles was saying the Egyptians had nothing to fear. He added: *Such cynicism towards allies destroys true partnership. It leaves only the choice of parting, or a master and vassal relationship.*[33]

But the Americans weren't alone in opposing his military plans. The UK Joint Intelligence Committee had warned within days of the canal nationalisation that 'we do not believe that threats of armed intervention ... would bring about the downfall of the Nasser regime or cause it to cancel the nationalisation'.[34] Divisions were emerging within the Cabinet. While Macmillan appeared as militant as ever – despite Treasury warnings about the dangers to sterling – the Minister of Defence, Walter Monckton, was warning against 'any premature recourse to force' while Butler, as William Clark put it, was 'a very damp influence'.[35] Labour had greatly moderated its early pro-war tone. The country was clearly divided. Lord Poole, the Conservative Party chairman, warned that 'liberal' opinion, which Eden had so decisively wooed to the Conservatives in 1951, felt strongly against military action. Perhaps most important, the canal was operating smoothly. Egyptian pilots, with East European help, were putting through as many ships as before nationalisation, and Nasser had made no move to molest British or French vessels.

If Eden had not at first seen force merely as a last resort, he began to do so now. The invasion date, originally 8 September, began to slip. The proposed landings were switched from Alexandria to Port Said, thus largely ruling out the direct overthrow of Nasser (though Eden thought any kind of defeat would probably bring him down) and necessitating further delay for revised plans. It was increasingly clear that the nationalisation of the canal alone was not a sufficient cause of war in the eyes of the world or of much of Britain. 'Eden could not at this juncture,' wrote Nutting, 'see how it would be possible to use force, unless Nasser struck the first blow.

And Nasser was showing no sign of obliging him.'[36] For these reasons, Eden agreed to a third channel for peaceful resolution: the UN.

It is not quite right to argue that Eden was determined on war and intended just to go through the motions at the UN. If a satisfactory settlement had been available there, he would have taken it. But his criteria for satisfaction were rigorous. He would not allow Nasser any face-saving formula. Since he regarded Nasser as a menace, and an untrustworthy one at that, the solution had to be harsh enough at least to undermine his prestige, if not bring him down. Then he could do no further harm even if he were minded to. Moreover, Eden did not want negotiations spun out. For one thing, the troops were ready and would become restless if kept waiting. For another, he feared a delay might allow Nasser to make a formal defence pact with the Soviets. And if there were voices pressing him to negotiate, there were equally powerful voices for immediate action. The French were raring to go. Macmillan, according to Clark, made 'a fairly clear, though reasonably polite, threat to resign'.[37] The annual Conservative party conference was due, where a bellicose mood was certain.

So it is equally wrong to suggest that Eden was now set on a peaceful outcome. The truth is that, as so often in his life, he was vacillating. His faith in American support was further damaged on 2 October when Dulles told a press conference that the US 'cannot be expected to identify itself 100 per cent ... with the colonial powers'.[38] Eden told the *Times* correspondent Iverach McDonald, who was close to him throughout the crisis: *How on earth can you work with people like that? It leaves us in a quite impossible situation. We can't go on like this.*[39]

But Lloyd went to the UN in early October in a positive frame of mind, and the Egyptians proved more amenable than anybody expected. They agreed to six principles for running the canal including that the dues should be settled by agreement between the users and the Egyptians and that 'the operation of the canal should be insulated from the politics of any country'. In Nutting's view, they too had been under political and economic pressure and were 'willing to negotiate an agreement which gave the maritime powers substantially all that they were asking'.[40] Lloyd wrote to Eden that 'the results are better than we were justified in expecting before we came'.[41] Eisenhower told a press conference that 'a very great crisis ... is behind us'.[42]

But Eden wanted specific and immediate proposals from the Egyptians on how the principles would be implemented. Otherwise, they *just flapped in the air* and *the way was open to endless procrastination*. When Lloyd put a resolution to this effect before the Security Council, the Russians vetoed it. As Eden told it in his memoirs, he now believed that, as a result of the veto, all the proposals for a peaceful way out were dead. *It was no use to fool ourselves ... We had been strung along over many months ... from pretext to pretext, from device to device, from contrivance to contrivance. At each stage in this weary pilgrimage we had seen our position weakened.*[43] Yet on receiving news of the veto, on the morning of Sunday 14 October, he cabled Lloyd proposing that Britain and France try to persuade the Egyptians to attend a conference, possibly in Geneva. Lloyd himself still thought an agreement with the Egyptians was possible, perhaps within a week. But later that day, a French delegation arrived at Chequers to put forward a quite different plan which would launch the final and decisive stage of the crisis. It was to involve Israel and it would, as Lloyd's private secretary later put it, 'foreclose the peaceful approach'.[44]

The idea had been lurking in the background all along. At the beginning of August, Macmillan had proposed that Israel should be encouraged to attack Egypt. The French, always doubtful about British resolve, had themselves approached the Israelis in early September and the British probably knew of these talks. Now, the impatient French, despairing of the British ever biting the bullet, wanted the Israelis to go ahead. But the Israelis wanted somebody to take out the Egyptian air force to protect their cities from retaliation. Only the British had sufficient bombers.

So the plan was that Israel would attack Egypt across the Sinai Desert. At a suitable moment, the British and French would call for both sides to withdraw from the Canal Zone. If Egypt refused, as she almost certainly would, Anglo-French forces would intervene. Here was the pretext for sending troops to Egypt that Eden needed. At that time, there was no threat to free passage through the canal; an Israeli invasion and subsequent fighting would create one. Better still, the 1954 treaty allowed to Britain to re-occupy the Canal Zone in an emergency. Nutting, who was at Chequers that day, thought Eden made his mind up there and then. When Nutting proposed consulting FO lawyers, Eden replied: *The lawyers are always against our doing anything. For God's sake, keep them out of it.*[45]

The lawyers are always against our doing anything. For God's sake, keep them out of it.

EDEN

Eden may now have hoped that he could just await the Israeli attack. But the Israelis, probably wisely, wanted a firmer commitment, and they wanted to hear it from British lips. So Lloyd flew secretly on 22 October to Sèvres, a villa near Paris, to meet David Ben-Gurion, the Israeli premier, Moshe Dayan, the Israeli chief of staff, and Shimon Peres of the Israeli defence ministry. According to Dayan, 'his whole demeanour expressed distaste'[46] – as well it might, since what could have been passed off as a gentlemanly agreement to act in hypothetical circumstances was about to become a plot. Lloyd was insistent that Britain must not appear as an aggressor with foreknowledge of the Israeli attack. The difficulty was that, if Britain bombed Egyptian airfields too early, that was exactly how she would appear. But the Israelis wanted Nasser's air force taken out before Tel Aviv was reduced to rubble. On this difficulty, the talks broke up and Eden told the Cabinet on 23 October: *It now seemed unlikely that the Israelis would launch a full scale attack.*[47]

But that day, Foreign Office officials were sent back to Sèvres with instructions, in effect, to split the difference on the timing of the air raids. Lloyd himself didn't go, because he was scheduled to answer questions in the Commons that afternoon and his absence might arouse suspicion. The plan was agreed, with dates and details of the ultimatum that the British and French would issue, ostensibly to both sides. Secrecy was also agreed, for all time. At the end, the FO officials signed a document, which became known as the Sèvres Protocol. When Eden heard that such a document existed, the officials were sent back to Paris to destroy the French and Israeli copies. They failed. No trace of the British copy has ever been found. Nor is there any copy in the British archives of a letter that Eden wrote to Guy Mollet, the French prime minister, stating: *Her Majesty's Government have been informed of the conversations held at Sèvres ... They confirm that in the situation there envisaged they will take the action described.*[48]

The charge that a plot had been hatched was made almost as soon as the invasion took place a few days later, and evidence as to its nature trickled out over the following years. Though Eden lied to the Commons, specifically denying collusion in his last speech on 20 December 1956, he kept the Cabinet far better informed than its members later claimed. He never told them the full nature of the conspiracy, but he said enough to have prompted, among supposedly intelligent men of the world, more questions than they ever asked. He specifically talked of *secret conversations* with the Israelis. Outlining what 'might' happen and how Britain would then act, he said *we must face the risk that we shall be accused of collusion* but *we should never have a better pretext for intervention against him* [Nasser] *than we have now.*[49]

However, in his memoirs, published in 1960, Eden omitted any mention of Sévres or of any talks with the Israelis. Lloyd's account, published 18 years later, admitted to the Sévres meeting, but was less than honest about its nature. 'I do not myself believe,' he wrote (a very odd choice of words), 'that there was any binding agreement between the Israeli and British Governments.'[50] The FO officials, he insisted, had merely signed a record of the discussions. Even Eden's most sympathetic biographers find it hard to excuse a plot that seemed designed purely to get him out of a desperate political corner. Eden himself referred many years later to *our twisted plans.*[51] There is only one plausible defence, though Eden merely hinted at it in his memoirs. Israel was then suffering cross-border commando raids from both Jordan and Egypt. She was minded to retaliate somehow. But an attack on Jordan would have thrown Britain, and even the Western Alliance, into complete confusion. Britain was committed by a 1948 treaty to helping Jordan. The extraordinary situation could have arisen where Britain was obliged to fight alongside a Soviet-armed Egypt against France and Israel. *This nightmare*, Eden later wrote in his diary, *haunted me.*[52] Perhaps so, but it seems an inadequate explanation for such duplicity.

Once the agreement with the Israelis was sealed, Eden's tiredness and bad temper, according to several witnesses, temporarily disappeared. *We've got an agreement!* he told the

Chief Whip Edward Heath, describing it as *the highest form of statesmanship*.[53] On 29 October, the Israelis attacked. The following day, the Anglo-French ultimatum, asking each side to withdraw 10 miles either side of the Canal Zone, was issued as agreed. Given the positions of the two armies at the time, the effect was to invite the Israelis to advance 115 miles while the Egyptians retreated 135 miles. The world was amazed. Even British diplomats and Commonwealth prime ministers had little or no warning. The leader of Britain's UN delegation described the effort of 'putting a plausible and confident face on the case' as 'the severest moral and physical strain I have ever experienced'. Clark was 'completely flabbergasted' and thought at once 'that all this was a deep-laid plot of some age'. Shuckburgh, who had the left the FO for the Imperial Defence College, but knew Eden and foreign policy realities better than most people, had expected the Israelis to be allowed to 'chew up Nasser's army a bit' before Britain joined the US in condemning the attack. He was 'staggered' by the Anglo-French ultimatum and wrote in his diary: 'We are about to be at war without the nation or Parliament having been given a hint of it ... A.E. has gone off his head.'[54]

> 'We are about to be at war without the nation or Parliament having been given a hint of it ... A.E. has gone off his head.'
>
> EVELYN SHUCKBURGH

Most amazed of all were the Americans. 'Nobody,' wrote Nutting, 'was kept more completely in the dark than the President of the United States.'[55] Even Eden's telegram informing him of the forthcoming ultimatum failed to arrive before it became public. Eisenhower was furious: 'I feel I must urgently express to you my deep concern at ... this drastic action,' he wrote. At the Security Council, Britain and France vetoed an American resolution calling for Israeli withdrawal from Egypt. Gaitskell called the veto 'an act of disastrous folly whose tragic consequences we shall regret for years'.[56]

RAF bombing of airfields and military targets began on the evening of 31 October. 'Britain is at war with Egypt,' announced the *Daily Mail* front page the next morning. The country was in uproar. 'The scenes in the House of Commons,' wrote Robert Rhodes James who, as a young Commons clerk, watched from the gallery, 'were beyond modern precedent.'[57] The sitting had to be suspended for the first time since 1924. A Gallup poll found 44 per cent of Britons were against the military action, and only 37 per cent for it. Though no announcements were made immediately, Eden knew two ministers, including Nutting, had resigned, as had William Clark. Lord Mountbatten, the First Sea Lord, was teetering on the edge of resignation, writing (in green ink) on 2 November 'I feel so desperate about what is happening'.[58] A fortnight earlier, Monckton had been moved from Defence to another ministry because of his doubts. 'It seems to me,' Clark wrote in his diary, 'that the PM is mad, literally mad.'[59]

In New York, the UN General Assembly, in the first emergency session it had ever held, voted overwhelmingly for the withdrawal of British, French and Israeli forces with only those three countries, plus Australia and New Zealand, voting against. *It was not Soviet Russia, or any Arab state, but the Government of the United States which took the lead*, recalled Eden bitterly. Soviet troops were at the same time speeding towards Budapest to put down an anti-communist rebellion. In Eden's view, US dilatoriness in pushing a denunciation of this invasion through the UN *provided a damaging contrast to the alacrity they were showing in arraigning the French and ourselves*.[60] The extent to which the Americans opposed the invasion became dramatically clearer when the US Sixth Fleet began to harass the Anglo-French task force on its journey towards Port Said. For a terrible moment, it seemed intent on physically intervening, and challenging the task force to shoot down a US aircraft or sink a submarine. In the opinion of the Anglo-French commander, 'both these might easily have happened' if his officers 'had not shown patience and care of the highest order'.[61]

With the landings imminent, Eden broadcast to the nation on 3 November. *All my life*, he said, *I've been a man of peace ... I've been a League of Nations man and a United Nations man and I'm still the same man, with the same convictions ... I couldn't be other if I wished.* Christopher Chancellor, the normally impassive chairman of Reuter's news agency, hurled his whisky glass at the television screen. 'We had not realised,' said the *Observer* in an editorial the following morning, 'that our Government was capable of such folly and such crookedness.'[62]

> 'We had not realised that our Government was capable of such folly and such crookedness.'
>
> THE OBSERVER

That Sunday, ministers met as Labour's Aneurin Bevan addressed a rally in nearly Trafalgar Square, creating, recalled Lloyd, 'a steady hum of noise and then every few minutes a crescendo and an outburst of howling or booing'.[63] The pressure on Eden was intense. Lloyd reported that oil sanctions against Britain and France were being proposed at the UN. 'That finishes it!' wailed Macmillan, throwing his hands in the air.[64] But it didn't, even though what Eden called *the weaker sisters* in the Cabinet now showed their hand. When news of a likely ceasefire between Egypt and Israel arrived, several ministers suggested that, since the demands of the ultimatum had been met, it would be absurd for Britain to land troops. Others thought it would be absurd not to, when the whole object of British policy was to get back control of the Canal. Eden certainly mentioned resignation at one point, though Butler's claim that he told the Cabinet 'he must go upstairs and consider his position' is disputed, as is a political journalist's claim that he broke down in tears and cried 'you are all deserting me'.[65] When it was later reported that there would be no ceasefire after all, 'everyone,' according to Clarissa Eden's diary, 'laughed and banged the table with relief'.[66] Yet it was the Israelis who had rejected a ceasefire. Britain's position was more absurd than ever. Israel had invaded and now refused to withdraw. To curb her, Britain would next day land troops on Egyptian beaches to fight Egyptian soldiers. This was surely the strangest police action in history.

After two days, it was all over. On 6 November, Macmillan told the Cabinet of a run on the pound. Britain had lost 15 per cent of her gold and currency reserves in less than a week and the country faced ruin, he said. There is no evidence that Treasury officials put it as dramatically as that – or, at any rate, no more dramatically than they expressed previous warnings to Macmillan – and the loss of reserves later turned out to be about a third of what Macmillan claimed. But for whatever reason the Chancellor had phoned Washington for help. He was told he would get it only if British forces accepted a ceasefire by midnight.

Macmillan, previously the most gung-ho minister, was now adamant for a ceasefire. So were Butler and Salisbury, the other most senior ministers. Only three Cabinet members wanted to continue. Eden, too tired and stressed to fight on, had to agree. Britain was humiliated, the French furious at her perfidy. As Eden announced the decision to the Commons, a Labour MP thought 'the whole personality, if not prostrated, seemed completely withdrawn'.[67]

The canal could have been taken within five days, and perhaps as little as 48 hours. Dulles, in hospital for a cancer operation at the height of the crisis, later asked Lloyd: 'Why did you stop? Why didn't you go through with it and get Nasser down?'[68] Eden, when preparing his memoirs, remarked that *why we stopped is going to be more difficult to explain than why we started.*[69] Many complex explanations have been advanced, including the suggestion that ministers feared a Soviet invasion of Syria or took seriously Khrushchev's threat to bombard London

Why we stopped is going to be more difficult to explain than why we started.

EDEN

with rockets. But the simplest explanation is best. Britain, a maritime trading nation with a reserve currency, could not afford to stand alone against the world. The fighting between Israel and Egypt had stopped, with the latter overwhelmed. The UN had agreed to send in a peacekeeping force, albeit without British or French troops. The ostensible purpose of the Anglo-French ultimatum had been achieved. A subterfuge allowed to Eden to invade Egypt; the same subterfuge compelled him to come out.

After the ceasefire, Eden wrote in his diary, the US *insisted in rubbing our noses in it.*[70] He hoped British troops might stay to clear the canal, which Nasser had blocked when the fighting started. But they weren't allowed even to do that. The UN General Assembly, with American support, voted to censure Britain and France and demanded an immediate and unconditional withdrawal. Macmillan, warning of the continuing dangers to sterling and oil supplies, was adamant it must be obeyed. The humiliation was complete. Lloyd announced it to MPs on 3 December. It was, recalled Rhodes James, 'a terrible occasion'.[71]

By then, Eden was far away. His health had been worrying his doctors for some time, following a severe fever which had put him in London's University College Hospital for a weekend in early October. On 23 November, with Britain

The Hungarian Revolution, 1956

When on 30 October 1956 Imre Nagy, the symbol of liberalisation and reform policies, was asked to form a government, this was done in the vain hope of quelling the fighting and rioting, which had broken out the previous week. On the same day that Nagy's new government took office, Moscow released a major policy statement, which took a conciliatory position with respect to the Hungarian situation and affirmed that the Soviet Union and the satellites could 'build their mutual relations only on the principles of complete equality ... and of non-interference in one another's internal affairs'. It did, however, also contain the threat that the Soviet Union would not allow any of its satellites to abandon the supremacy of Communist Party or to secede from its sphere of influence.

In spite of the statement's explicit promise to withdraw Soviet troops from Hungary, however, by 1 November no move had been made to do so. Nagy became convinced that the Soviets had no intention of following through on their declaration. As a result, he ignored the clear warning contained in the declaration and announced Hungary's neutrality, and asked the United Nations to consider means of aiding the Hungarians in their struggle. With this move, Nagy overstepped what had been set as the permissible limits of behaviour for a socialist country.' On the morning of 4 November the hopes of the Hungarians were shattered as Soviet troops again invaded Budapest in full force. Nagy appealed for Western aid to protect Hungary's neutrality. The Soviet forces soon overran the city, Nagy's government fell and a new regime headed by Janos Kadar took over.

During the most critical period of the Hungarian revolution – the seven days directly preceding the second massive Soviet intervention on 4 November – events in Hungary were overshadowed by another crisis: Suez. The serious rift between the United States and its two major Western allies over Egypt could not have come at a worse time for Hungary and a better time for the leaders of the Soviet Union as it diverted the attention of the United States and the United Nations away from Europe and consequently decreased the chances of Western action being taken in support of the Nagy government.

in the grip of petrol rationing, he left for a complete rest in Jamaica, 'an island much patronised by tax evaders and affluent idlers', as one contemporary observed.[72] Butler was left in charge. From the day Eden flew out it was clear to most that his premiership could not survive. The Americans were certainly led to believe it couldn't, mainly by Macmillan. Whether, as some accounts claim, Eden's resignation was a condition of their continuing support for British finances is far more doubtful. What is true is that Eisenhower put Eden in the deep freeze. 'He wouldn't even communicate with him,' recalled the US ambassador in London.[73]

Yet in Britain, opinion had swung in favour of the military action and Eden's personal popularity remained high. Robert Allan, his PPS, cabled that 'your position is unimpaired'. When Eden returned to London in mid-December, however, he found political power had drained from him. 'Everyone looking at us with thoughtful eyes,' recorded Clarissa in her diary. Eden's senior ministers virtually dictated what he said to the press, vetoing any further references to Nasser's dictatorial ambitions. When he returned to the Commons, he must have known it was over. 'Eden slipped into the House virtually without any attention being paid to him,' recalled the watching Rhodes James. 'One Conservative MP ... leaped to his feet and waved his order paper; he looked around him, was stunned by the pervasive silence on the Conservative benches, and subsided with a thunderstruck look ... Eden looked hard at his shoes, and his colleagues shuffled papers.' At a New Year Cabinet meeting, one official 'saw in his eyes a man pursued by every demon'.

The doctors enabled him to go with a modicum of dignity. After seeking three eminent opinions, he got a unanimous verdict: 'his health will no longer enable him to sustain the heavy burdens inseparable from the office of Prime Minister'.

On 9 January 1957, he told the Cabinet: *I do not think I should be serving the best interests of my colleagues or the country if I were to continue in my present condition.*[74]

Later that day, he drove to Buckingham Palace to submit his resignation formally to the Queen. In the 20th century, only Andrew Bonar Law and Sir Alec Douglas-Home served for shorter periods as Prime Minister. Salisbury was charged with finding a successor. With his aristocratic lisp, he asked each member of the Cabinet: 'Is it to be Wab or Hawold?' It was to be Hawold, the man who was 'first in, first out' in the Suez adventure.

Part Three

THE LEGACY

Chapter 8: Conclusion: 1956–77

The word 'tragedy' is much overused. But Anthony Eden's life surely deserves the word. Nobody ever waited so long for the supreme prize in British politics; Lady Violet Bonham-Carter was right to say that 'to be P.M. was his life's one aim'.[1] Nobody ever worked so diligently to achieve his ambition. Nobody ever entered Downing Street with so much public respect or with such a track record of achievement in government office. And few reached the top in politics with such a blameless reputation. Not for him the devious plotting to which many others would have resorted in order to bring down Churchill. By the standards of his class, he was never well-off, but nobody could accuse him of profiting from political office – on the contrary, when he resumed office in 1951, he sold oil shares at their lowest point in the market, though ministers were not then required to do so.

Had Eden retired at the end of 1954, or fallen under the proverbial bus, he would – subject to the usual swings of historical revision – be hailed as one of the great Foreign Secretaries, alongside Palmerston and his contemporary Ernest Bevin. Instead, he is remembered as one of the worst Prime Ministers, fit to be bracketed with Lord North, who lost the American colonies. And his precipitous fall from grace – essentially a period of a few months after Nasser's nationalisation, since the troubles of his previous year could have turned out to be no more than the usual ups and downs of politics – was caused not by misfortune but by fatal flaws in his own character.

Only in one sense did Eden's life fall short of the classical Greek tragedy: even on the eve of death, self-knowledge never came to him. He never repented of Suez and he spent much of the rest of his life talking about it. Though he gave up his Commons seat immediately on leaving office, he at first refused an earldom, believing the nation might one day recall him to glory. 'He always thinks in the back of his mind that the miracle will happen,' wrote his wife. He finally became Earl of Avon in 1961, accepting he would never return to the Commons. Yet Anthony Montague Browne, Churchill's private secretary, recalled swimming with him that year in the Caribbean: 'For some twenty minutes he talked of that disaster [Suez], now from the trough of a wave, now from the peak. It was obsessive, but also eloquent and touching.'[2] As late as 1976, Henry Brandon, the *Sunday Times* Washington correspondent, meeting Eden at a dinner, found him pleading for 'justice before history'. As Brandon put it, 'the ghost of Suez was still stalking Eden as he was getting ready for the end'.[3]

The end was indeed close. Eden died from cancer of the liver on 14 January 1977, five months short of his 80th birthday, 20 years and five days after he had left Downing Street, two months after a Labour Cabinet had finally accepted that Britain could no longer determine even her own economic policy. The last two decades of his life had been uneventful, punctuated by four volumes of memoirs, occasional speeches in the Lords, reviews of books related to Suez or appeasement, the breeding of Hereford cattle, and an active presidency of the Royal Shakespeare Company. There were also continued bouts of ill-health. In 1965, acting as a pallbearer at Churchill's funeral, he looked, wrote the Labour minister Richard Crossman, 'literally ashen grey ... It felt like the end of an epoch, possibly even the end of a nation'.[4]

Could that end have been delayed if Eden had been allowed to see through his ambition to overthrow Nasser? Many thought the brutal overthrow of the pro-British regime in Iraq in 1958 proved his warnings right, and almost every subsequent development in the Middle East – the 1967 and 1973 Arab-Israeli wars, the 1970s 'oil shock' to Western economies, the rise of Saddam Hussein and his invasion of Kuwait in 1990, right down to the present rise of Islamic fundamentalism – is adduced by some as evidence of Eden's prescience. Others argue that his unprovoked attack on Egypt, and his collusion with Israel, did much to create the anti-Western distrust, shading into hatred, that now dominates the region.

None of this takes us very far. The truth is that Eden, born in the year of Queen Victoria's Diamond Jubilee, belonged to a generation that believed countries inhabited by darker-skinned races could and should be moulded in the West's interests generally and in Britain's interests in particular. Unlike Churchill, he was not so foolish as to believe the British could continue to rule India, and he was generally sympathetic to colonies' rights to self-determination. But he expected continued deference to Western strategic and economic interests. Inferior nations could rule themselves only if they did as they were told, much as the workers could have their unions if they didn't upset the established social and economic order. Like many of his generation and class, Eden believed British rule was uniquely benevolent. Britain was a kind of aristocrat among nations, and her leadership could deliver peace and stability. Upstart nations, such as the Italians, for whom, according to one observer, he had 'strong antipathy, almost physical repulsion',[5] were not to fit to rule others. That was why he was so uncompromising in his approach to Mussolini, who had imperial ambitions beyond Europe, and to Nasser, who wished to dominate the Middle East. Hitler, by contrast, had no ambitions beyond Europe (despite British attempts to buy him off with colonies) and Stalin's ambitions, too, were mostly in countries that bordered his own. Besides, Germany and Russia were historically great nations, with claims to aristocratic, martial virtues. The Americans might have money but they were upstarts, and vulgar ones at that. Eden was doubly wrong. The Americans were no more likely to recognise the merits of British leadership than were Egyptians or Indians. It was they rather than the British who could now aspire to impose their will on the world. And they too would come to believe that their leadership was uniquely benevolent. The results were no happier. The world in which the white races, whatever their leadership, could mould other countries without serious challenge was passing.

As Eden's press adviser, a distinguished diplomatic correspondent, put it: 'Eden was only a blip in the shedding of Empire. Within six months of Suez we had started ... decolonization in Africa.'[6] Macmillan, while Chancellor, had grasped the extent of British weakness; he also understood that any hurt pride among the British could be soothed by telling them they had 'never had it so good'. As the playwright Denis Potter recorded, a young miner in the Forest of Dean might remark that 'this country is not capable of it any more – not even against the bloody wogs'.[7] But why should he care, if he could now afford a washing machine for his wife?

'Eden was only a blip in the shedding of Empire. Within six months of Suez we had started ... decolonization in Africa.'

WILLIAM CLARK

Eden's premiership

'It was within his own Cabinet Room and the Whitehall machine over which he presided that Eden aroused serious doubts about his temperament, his judgment and his poor health long before Suez. For Eden was the greatest fusser to have filled the premiership probably of the last century; certainly since 1945.

Yet as prime minister, Eden meant well. He tried to accommodate and reassure his ministers. He imitated Baldwin, under whom he came to his political maturity, by inviting colleagues to Downing Street to chat *à deux* about their departments. But unlike those of his model, Baldwin, or Labour's latter-day Baldwin, Jim Callaghan, who revived the practice 20 years later, Eden's sessions were occasions to be endured rather than enjoyed. As Robert Rhodes James put it, "it is fair to say that British Prime Ministers tend to fall into one of two categories – the Olympian and the interferer. From almost the day he entered Downing Street, Eden was the latter." ... Initially this counterproductive impulse might have been seen as a consequence of Eden's not creating the Cabinet he wanted until the reshuffle of December 1955 (a delay in stamping his own mark on Whitehall that he came to regret). But this was not so. It was almost congenital and continued long after the reshuffle and right through to his last days in No. 10.

Of course, it was not just a question of nerves. He was ill. According to Dr Hugh L'Etang (who was until his death the leading scholar of the pathology of leadership), Eden was suffering from 'the toxic effects of bile duct infection, and the chemical effects of stimulant and possibly other medication': benzedrine was almost certainly a factor here. Add to the effect of the benzedrine poor sleep and the desperate need for a holiday as the 1955–6 session of Parliament drew to a close, and you have a cocktail of mania-inducing qualities. These were ready-mixed at the precise moment, if Lloyd's Minister of State at the Foreign Office, Anthony Nutting, is to be believed, when Colonel Nasser took his dramatic action on the night of 26 July 1956.'

(Hennessy, The Prime Minister, pp 213–215)

Unlike Munich (and, for that matter, the sterling crisis of 1976), Suez left few permanent marks on Britain. It was scarcely mentioned in the 1959 general election, which the Conservatives won comfortably. Once the Suez Canal was cleared, oil flowed freely and, a decade later, the amount of shipping passing through had doubled. Anglo-American relations returned to an even keel and became closer – too close for some tastes – as the years passed. De Gaulle's vetoes in 1963 and 1967 on British membership of the European Community may in part be traced back to Suez and the way Britain pulled out in response to American commands. But the French distrust of perfidious Albion long predated Suez and, once de Gaulle had gone, the British duly joined Europe. Suez has often been described as a disaster for Britain. It wasn't; it was just a disaster for Eden.

The premiership exposed what Westminster, Whitehall and Fleet Street had always suspected: he was a political lightweight. The Tory MP Henry Channon, writing in 1951, thought him the nicest and most civilised man in the Commons, but 'he is, always has been, and ever will be, a lightweight'.[8] He appeared all the more so because he emerged from Churchill's shadow. 'Both as a judge of men and as a cool appraiser of events,' wrote Charles Moran, Churchill's doctor, 'Anthony is much sounder and more discriminating than Winston, but the personality of the P.M. and his power over words raise him into another world, which will always be closed to Anthony, who was born, and will remain, a secondary figure.'[9]

Eden had hardly any power over words, in public at least. His popularity rested on his good looks and his good clothes – 'no man,' Butler said, 'could wear a grey suit better'[10] – and on his patent sincerity. But as Channon observed in 1943, 'he had not the gift of holding the House [of Commons]'.[11]

His gift was for platitudinous bromides, which could work well on radio and TV but not with live audiences. His aides were sometimes reduced to despair by his habit of cutting any witticism or dramatic phrase from his speeches. After seeing Eden's draft of a speech, an aide ironically proposed that he should add his intention to leave 'no stone unturned'. Eden gratefully accepted the suggestion. He lacked, as Clark observed, 'any trace of a sense of humour'.[12]

'No man could wear a grey suit better.'

R A BUTLER ON EDEN

He was, above all, a plodder. His appetite for work was extraordinary and what he lacked in intellectual brilliance and imagination he made up for in grasp of detail. It was this diligence, allied to his smooth charm, which made him such a good diplomat. Few international conferences passed without some fulsome tribute to his skills. A Swedish envoy observed that he 'could change the atmosphere ... from deep pessimism and general mistrust to mild optimism and will-ingness to co-operate'.[13] Alexander Cadogan of the Foreign Office wrote: 'I don't think any Secretary of State I served excelled him in finesse, or as a negotiator, or in knowledge of foreign affairs.'[14]

But if he was a skilled, hard-working diplomat, he was also a control freak, incapable of delegation. During the war, he complained not just about Churchill interfering in foreign policy but also about several other ministers, including his own juniors. He was, wrote Labour's Hugh Dalton, 'like the little boy trying to clutch all the toys'.[15] Perhaps more important, his diplomatic persona tended to spill over into his wider political behaviour. An American state department official, observing him at a conference in 1954, noted that 'Eden was quick, he was skilful, he was eloquent in debate'. But 'in any conflict, in any collision, great or small', the instinct to find a compromise came naturally to him. He was uncomfortable with, perhaps even afraid of, confrontation – and that may be traced to his childhood and to his alarming father. Time and again, conversations with friends, family and subordinates reveal his unhappiness with Chamberlain or Churchill, and his determination to have it out with them. But nearly always, he drew back from making clear to them what he really thought and he rarely expressed his opinions openly in Cabinet. Chamberlain complained that he would 'always agree in theory, but always disagree in practice'.[16] As a backbench MP, imploring Eden to do something about the plight of the European Jews in 1944, Harold Nicolson expressed a similar frustration: 'One goes away thinking how reasonable, how agreeable and how helpful he has been, and then discovers that in fact he has promised nothing at all.'[17]

Worse still, the affability concealed a vile temper, which may itself explain Eden's fear of confrontation. 'This defect,' wrote Clark, 'was one of the best-kept secrets about Eden. I heard not a whisper of its existence until I went to Downing Street; he enjoyed a public reputation ... as the most considerate, charming and calm of men. But in private, under pressure and hostility, he used to become perfectly terrible.'[18] One senior British diplomat compared him to an Arab horse: 'he used to get terribly het up and excited and he had to be sort of kept down.'[19] It is to Eden's credit that his tantrums were quickly forgotten and soon followed by apologies. Shuckburgh compared him to a child. 'You can have a scene with a child of great violence with angry words spoken ... and ten minutes later the whole thing is forgotten.'[20] It is less to Eden's credit that subordinates suffered the brunt of his temper more often than his superiors.

Was his temper caused by his chronic ill-health? Or was it the other way round? The best answer is that each fed off the other. Eden's numerous bodily complaints included ulcers, which are commonly associated with stress. He was, by any standards, a restless, highly-strung man: 'always very excitable, very feminine-type, very easily upset, easily annoyed', as Macmillan put it.[21] His excessive working hours didn't help. In March 1936, Nicolson, seeing him at a party, thought he 'looked haggard with exhaustion, his lovely eyes rimmed with red and puffy with sleeplessness'.[22] The 1953 operations damaged his bile duct and, by Suez, he was literally bilious. Most ministers agree that the pain, the sleepless nights, the fevers and the drugs he had to take clouded his judgement.

Eden might have been a better politician and more relaxed human being, less ready to take offence, if he had enjoyed more close personal relationships. But he lost his closest brother and his elder son, his eccentric mother was emotionally distant, and his first marriage was never truly happy. Nor was he the clubbable sort. He avoided the London clubs and for the Commons and its heavily masculine atmosphere he had 'an invincible distaste'.[23] 'One ought to spend an hour a day in the smoke-room,' Churchill told him in 1945. *I suppose so, but I don't like it*, replied Eden.[24] His failure to cultivate a political following at Westminster almost certainly delayed his accession to the premiership and perhaps hastened the end of his career.

He did not care much for the wider Conservative Party. Though no great brain himself – indeed, he despised intellectuals – he couldn't abide people he thought ignorant and backward-looking. He was most at ease, he always insisted, with ordinary working people and soldiers. This shy and deeply insecure man probably liked such company because it allowed him to feel secure in his social superiority. He knew where he stood when he met trade unionists or inspected soldiers. After a wartime meeting with trade unionists, he wrote in his diary, *I am infinitely happier among these folk than in the Carlton Club* [a traditional Tory club].[25] After a regimental visit, an officer wrote; 'I have never seen any inspecting VIP, military or civilian, who displayed ... the unerring touch that Eden had with troops ... he talked to every man in the front and rear rank of my Company.'[26] As one contemporary observed, Eden lived in a strange island, marooned in a world of superiors and subordinates. He didn't recognise equals, because he didn't have the social skills to cope with them.

It is against this background that we have to assess what were sometimes startlingly progressive social views. During the war, he several times discussed with Harvey, apparently quite seriously, whether he should join the Labour Party, and he seems to have envisaged with equanimity the emergence of the Communist Party as the main parliamentary opposition. He told Churchill in 1941 that he *felt no desire to work with the Tory Party as now constituted after war*.[27] Allowances should be made for the times. The Conservatives, as a sole party, had not technically held office since 1929 and Britain was then in close wartime alliance with Soviet Russia. It wasn't unreasonable for a career politician to worry the Tories might be permanently out of office in the future. Yet Eden's record put him consistently on the 'one nation' Tory left. In his lifelong enthusiasm for a 'property-owning democracy' and for giving working people a stake in capitalism, some have seen a precursor of Thatcherism. But one of his greatest passions was for industrial partnership, with workers enjoying part-ownership and sharing decisions in the companies that employed them – an idea closer to the Christian democracy of post-war Germany than to anything Margaret Thatcher would have embraced.

Moreover, Eden was among the enthusiasts for the wartime Beveridge Report, setting out a blueprint for the Welfare State. But his inexperience on the home front, and his weak understanding of economics, prevented him ever stamping his views on domestic policy even in Downing Street. He was never good at the big picture. During the war, Harvey urged him to take a lead in talking about the country's future, but found him, on such matters, 'as hesitating as he is bold and certain when speaking of foreign affairs'.[28]

All these weaknesses in Eden – the ill health, the fragile temper, the fear that he was a lightweight and an indecisive one at that, the sensitivity to criticism, the feeling that he could never make an impact on the home front, the lack of close confidants – combined in 1956 to create a perfect storm in the conduct of the nation's affairs. Perhaps the most fatal weakness of all was Eden's vanity, a vanity that was fed by insecurity. That, to many contemporaries, was his biggest flaw. He was forever asking, after some speech or conference, how well he had done; formed a jealous dislike of nearly all his colleagues; and lived in mortal fear that somebody else was getting a better press or more of the limelight. Butler, with his sly humour, gave the most vivid description, recalling how, as he walked back to the FO with him from a Commons debate in 1941, 'everybody in the crowd bowed and smiled' while Eden was 'looking first to the right then to the left'.[29] Shuckburgh gave the bluntest summary. 'He can't really bear any conversation to take place which does not in some way bear upon himself, his politics, his popularity, his successes in the past or present.'[30]

'He {Eden} can't really bear any conversation to take place which does not in some way bear upon himself, his politics, his popularity, his successes in the past or present.'

EVELYN SHUCKBURGH

Eden's vanity was piqued in 1956. An agreement he had made with Nasser just two years earlier, against vehement Tory opposition, had come unstuck; his premiership was being criticised as indecisive and lacklustre; the dread word 'appeaser' was being used; and the unfavourable comparisons with Churchill were growing. Adversity tempts all political leaders into military action. The temptations for Eden, floundering in a job for which he had waited nearly 20 years, were all the greater.

Eden's most recent biographer quotes Shakespeare as a suitable epitaph on his life and posthumous reputation: 'Men's evil manners live in brass, their virtues we write in water.' There is justice in that. Yet Suez was more than a one-off disaster at the end of a long career of achievement. It seemed to nullify everything Eden had stood for: straight dealing; commitment to resolving conflict through international bodies; careful, patient diplomacy. He destroyed not just his political career but a carefully-crafted reputation built up over more than 20 years, and he destroyed it for all time. That was the tragedy of Anthony Eden.

NOTES

Chapter 1: Early Life and Career: 1897–1931

1. Anthony Eden, *Another World 1897–1917* (Doubleday, New York: 1977) p 39, hereafter Eden, *Another World*.
2. Eden, *Another World*, p 8.
3. Eden, *Another World*, p 35.
4. Eden, *Another World*, pp 108, 116.
5. Eden, *Another World*, p 88.
6. Eden, *Another World*, p 153.
7. Eden, *Another World*, pp 167–8, 86.
8. Robert Rhodes James, *Anthony Eden* (Weidenfeld and Nicolson, London: 1986) p 52
9. Rhodes James, *Eden*, p 57; D R Thorpe, *Eden* (Pimlico, London: 2003) p 45, hereafter Thorpe.
10. Rhodes James, *Eden*, p 55.
11. Thorpe, p 45.
12. Rhodes James, *Eden*, p 60.
13. Rhodes James, *Eden*, pp 83–4.
14. Thorpe, p 97.
15. The Earl of Avon, *The Eden Memoirs: Facing the Dictators* (Cassell, London: 1962) p 12, hereafter Avon, *Facing*.
16. Thorpe, p 108.
17. Rhodes James, *Eden*, p 104.
18. Avon, *Facing*, pp 15–18.

Chapter 2: 'The Blue-Eyed Boy': 1931–5

1. Avon, *Facing*, p 28.
2. Thorpe, p 117.
3. Avon, *Facing*, pp 241–2.

4. David Dutton, *Anthony Eden: A Life and Reputation* (Arnold, London: 1997) p 99, hereafter Dutton.
5. David Carlton, *Anthony Eden: A Biography* (Allen and Unwin, London, 1986) p 32, hereafter Carlton.
6. Carlton, p 87.
7. Dutton, p 109.
8. Thorpe, pp 120–1, Carlton, p 33.
9. Avon, *Facing*, p 33.
10. Avon, *Facing*, pp 45–7.
11. Ian Colvin, *Vansittart in Office* (Gollancz, London: 1965) pp 23–4.
12. Avon, *Facing*, p 57.
13. Avon, *Facing*, p 61.
14. Carlton, p 45, Thorpe, p 130.
15. Rhodes James, *Eden*, p 135.
16. Carlton, p 44.
17. Carlton, pp 47, 51.
18. Avon, *Facing*, pp 71, 83.
19. Avon, *Facing*, p 117.
20. Thorpe, p 136.
21. Avon, *Facing*, p 119.
22. Dutton, p 48.
23. Avon, *Facing*, p 135.
24. Thorpe, p 143.
25. Avon, *Facing*, pp 142–3.
26. Thorpe, p 144.
27. Avon, *Facing*, p 153.
28. Avon, *Facing*, p 162.
29. Avon, *Facing*, pp 175, 179.
30. John Charmley, *Chamberlain and the Lost Peace* (Papermac, London: 1989) p 37, hereafter Charmley.
31. Dutton, p 48.
32. Thorpe, p 151.

33. Avon, *Facing*, pp 216–19.
34. Thorpe, p 153.
35. Dutton, p 45.
36. Avon, *Facing*, p 243.
37. Avon, *Facing*, p 298.
38. Carlton, p 69.
39. Carlton, p 70.
40. Avon, *Facing*, p 310.
41. Avon, *Facing*, p 316.
42. William Clark, *From Three Worlds: Memoirs* (Sidgwick and Jackson, London: 1986) p 148, hereafter Clark.
43. Thorpe, p 167

Chapter 3: Foreign Secretary: 1936–8

1. David Dilks (ed), *The Diaries of Sir Alexander Cadogan, O.M., 1938–45* (Cassell, London: 1971) p 415, hereafter Dilks (ed), *Cadogan Diaries*.
2. Carlton, p 81.
3. Thorpe, p 167.
4. Avon, *Facing*, p 338.
5. Avon, *Facing*, p 366.
6. Carlton, p 79.
7. Avon, *Facing*, pp 387–8.
8. Avon, *Facing*, p 399.
9. Avon, *Facing*, p 433.
10. John Harvey (ed), *The Diplomatic Diaries of Oliver Harvey 1937–1940* (Collins, London: 1970) p 34.
11. Avon, *Facing*, p 446
12. A J P Taylor, *The Origins of the Second World War* (Penguin, London: 1964) p 174.
13. Dutton, pp 80–1.
14. Carlton, p 103.

15. Martin Gilbert and Richard Gott, *The Appeasers* (Weidenfeld and Nicolson, London: 1963) p 81.
16. Charmley, p 30.
17. Carlton, pp 105, 116.
18. Harvey (ed), *The Diplomatic Diaries of Oliver Harvey*, p 67; Charmley, p 37.
19. Carlton, p 108.
20. Avon, *Facing*, p 453.
21. Avon, *Facing*, p 452.
22. Rhodes James, *Eden*, p 178.
23. Dilks (ed), *Cadogan Diaries*, p 44.
24. Avon, *Facing*, pp 493, 498.
25. Avon, *Facing*, pp 508, 510.
26. Harvey (ed), *The Diplomatic Diaries of Oliver Harvey*, pp 415–7.
27. Avon, *Facing*, p 512.
28. Avon, *Facing*, p 514.
29. Carlton, p 119.
30. Thorpe, p 198.
31. Avon, *Facing*, p 555.
32. Avon, *Facing*, p 554.
33. Harvey (ed), *The Diplomatic Diaries of Oliver Harvey*, p 76.
34. Taylor, *Origins of the Second World War*, p 175.
35. Carlton, p 127.
36. Avon, *Facing*, p 579.
37. Avon, *Facing*, p 582.
38. Thorpe, p 206; Dutton, p 106.
39. The Earl of Birkenhead, *Halifax: the Life of Lord Halifax* (Hamish Hamilton, London: 1965) p 379.
40. Dutton, pp 107, 116.
41. Avon, *Facing*, p 596.

42. Harold Nicolson, *Diaries and Letters, 1930–39* (Collins, London: 1966) p 327.

43. Winston S Churchill, *The Second World War, Volume 1: The Gathering Storm* (Cassell, London: 1948) p 231; Harvey (ed), *The Diplomatic Diaries of Oliver Harvey*, p 103; Robert Rhodes James (ed), *Chips: The Diaries of Sir Henry Channon* (Weidenfeld and Nicolson, London: 1967) p 145, hereafter Rhodes James (ed), *Channon*; Birkenhead, *Halifax*, p 417.

Chapter 4: Munich and the 'Phoney War': 1938–40

1. Thorpe, p 211.
2. Duff Cooper, *Old Men Forget* (Rupert Hart-Davis, London: 1957) p 214.
3. Harvey (ed), *The Diplomatic Diaries of Oliver Harvey*, p 130.
4. Dutton, pp 125–6.
5. The Earl of Avon, *The Eden Memoirs: The Reckoning* (Cassell, London: 1965) p 28, hereafter Avon, *Reckoning*.
6. Carlton, p 142.
7. Avon, *Reckoning*, pp 29–30.
8. Carlton, p 140.
9. Harvey (ed), *The Diplomatic Diaries of Oliver Harvey*, p 216; Carlton, p 144.
10. Avon, *Reckoning*, p 51.
11. Avon, *Reckoning*, p 91.
12. Avon, *Reckoning*, p 91.
13. John Colville, *The Fringes of Power: Downing Street Diaries 1939–1955* (Phoenix, London: 2005) p 37.
14. Harvey (ed), *The Diplomatic Diaries of Oliver Harvey*, p 326
15. Avon, *Reckoning*, pp 97, 81.
16. Avon, *Reckoning*, p 103.

17. Thorpe, p 247.
18. Avon, *Reckoning*, pp 112, 117.
19. Avon, *Reckoning*, p 124.
20. Avon, *Reckoning*, pp 175, 131.
21. Avon, *Reckoning*, pp 169–70.
22. Avon, *Reckoning*, pp 183–7.
23. Dilks (ed), *Cadogan Diaries*, p 382.

Chapter 5: Wartime Foreign Secretary: 1941–5

1. Dutton, p 179.
2. John Harvey (ed), *The War Diaries of Oliver Harvey 1941–1945* (Collins, London: 1978) p 50.
3. Avon, *Reckoning*, p 190.
4. Dilks (ed), *Cadogan Diaries*, p 358.
5. Avon, *Reckoning*, p 192.
6. Dilks (ed), *Cadogan Diaries*, p 360.
7. Dutton, p 181.
8. Dilks (ed), *Cadogan Diaries*, p 361; Thorpe, p 259.
9. Avon, *Reckoning*, p 240.
10. Rhodes James (ed), *Channon*, pp 302–3.
11. Avon, *Reckoning*, p 366.
12. Dutton, p 187.
13. Avon, *Reckoning*, pp 286, 315.
14. Avon, *Reckoning*, pp 301–3.
15. Carlton p 192, Dutton, p 190.
16. Avon, *Reckoning*, p 318.
17. Dilks (ed), *Cadogan Diaries*, p 449.
18. Harvey (ed), *The War Diaries of Oliver Harvey*, pp 130–1.
19. Harvey (ed), *The War Diaries of Oliver Harvey*, p 100.
20. Thorpe, p 271.
21. Harvey (ed), *The War Diaries of Oliver Harvey*, pp 149–50.
22. Harvey (ed), *The War Diaries of Oliver Harvey*, p 187.

23. Avon, *Reckoning*, p 352.
24. Thorpe, p 275.
25. Dutton, p 152.
26. Harvey (ed), *The War Diaries of Oliver Harvey*, p 182.
27. Carlton, p 220; Dutton, p 143.
28. Thorpe, p 278.
29. Harvey (ed), *The War Diaries of Oliver Harvey*, p 271.
30. Avon, *Reckoning*, p 398.
31. Harvey (ed), *The War Diaries of Oliver Harvey*, p 274.
32. Harvey (ed), *The War Diaries of Oliver Harvey*, pp 248, 255.
33. Thorpe, p 289.
34. Avon, *Reckoning*, p 418.
35. Avon, *Reckoning*, p 429.
36. Avon, *Reckoning*, p 436.
37. Carlton, p 233.
38. Dutton, p 209.
39. Dutton, p 170.
40. Dilks (ed), *Cadogan Diaries*, p 635.
41. Avon, *Reckoning*, p 457.
42. Harold Nicolson, *Diaries and Letters, 1939–45* (Collins, London: 1967) p 412.
43. Dilks (ed), *Cadogan Diaries*, p 671.
44. Harvey (ed), *The War Diaries of Oliver Harvey*, p 365.
45. Lord Moran, *Winston Churchill: The Struggle for Survival 1940–1965* (Sphere, London: 1968) p 237, hereafter Moran.
46. Avon, *Reckoning*, p 481.
47. Carlton, pp 244–6.
48. Carlton, p 215.
49. Dutton, p 212.
50. Nicolson, *Diaries and Letters, 1939–45*, p 421.
51. Dilks (ed), *Cadogan Diaries*, p 717.

52. Avon, *Reckoning*, p 522.
53. Dilks (ed), *Cadogan Diaries*, pp 719, 765.
54. Harvey (ed), *The War Diaries of Oliver Harvey*, p 385.
55. Avon, *Reckoning*, p 549.
56. Thorpe, pp 312–13.
57. Rhodes James, *Eden*, p 304.
58. Dutton, pp 256, 230.
59. Avon, *Reckoning*, p 551.

Chapter 6: 'I do wish the old man would go': 1945–55

1. Dutton, p 231.
2. Avon, *Reckoning*, p 554.
3. Rhodes James, *Eden*, p 304.
4. Rhodes James, *Eden*, pp 327–8.
5. Thorpe, p 340.
6. Rhodes James, *Eden*, p 329.
7. Dutton, p 233.
8. Thorpe, p 343.
9. A J P Taylor, *Beaverbrook* (Penguin, London: 1974) p 770.
10. Carlton, p 295.
11. Rhodes James (ed), *Channon*, p 470; Dutton, p 244.
12. Evelyn Shuckburgh, *Descent to Suez: Diaries, 1951–56* (Weidenfeld and Nicolson, London: 1986) p 66, hereafter Shuckburgh.
13. Shuckburgh, p 14.
14. Rhodes James, *Eden*, p 597.
15. Carlton, pp 316–7.
16. Dutton, p 475.
17. Henry Pelling, *Churchill's Peacetime Ministry, 1951–55* (Macmillan, London: 1997) p 58.
18. Dutton, pp 304, 390.
19. Dutton, pp 169, 330.

20. Carlton, p 324.
21. Dutton, p 288.
22. Rhodes James, *Eden*, p 353.
23. Thorpe, p 367.
24. The Earl of Avon, *The Memoirs of Sir Anthony Eden: Full Circle* (Cassell, London: 1960) p 36, hereafter Avon, *Full Circle*.
25. Thorpe, p 412.
26. Avon, *Full Circle*, pp 77, 97.
27. Avon, *Full Circle*, p 93.
28. Carlton, p 344.
29. Avon, *Full Circle*, p 103.
30. Shuckburgh, pp 186–7.
31. Thorpe, p 393.
32. Avon, *Full Circle*, p 127.
33. Carlton, p 348.
34. Avon, *Full Circle*, p 124.
35. Dutton, p 348.
36. Avon, *Full Circle*, p 168.
37. Shuckburgh, p 6.
38. Avon, *Full Circle*, p 260.
39. Shuckburgh, pp 75–6; Avon, *Full Circle*, p 247.
40. Shuckburgh, p 95.
41. Dutton, p 358.
42. Thorpe, p 420.
43. Shuckburgh, p 110.
44. Avon, *Full Circle*, pp 256–7.
45. Shuckburgh, p 151.
46. Thorpe, p 421.
47. Rhodes James, *Eden*, p 393.
48. Thorpe, p 428.
49. Colville, p 660.
50. Moran, p 676.

51. Colville, p 662.

Chapter 7: Suez: 1955–6

1. Peter Hennessy, *The Prime Minister: The Office and its Holders since 1945* (Allen Lane, London: 2000) p 212, hereafter Hennessy.
2. Avon, *Full Circle*, p 281.
3. Rhodes James, *Eden*, p 405.
4. Carlton, p 376.
5. Dutton, p 479.
6. Shuckburgh, p 277.
7. Anthony Howard, *Rab: The Life of R A Butler* (Papermac, London: 1988), p 217, hereafter Howard.
8. Anthony Nutting, *No End of a Lesson: The Story of Suez* (Constable, London: 1996), p 25, hereafter Nutting.
9. Shuckburgh, pp 326, 330.
10. Rhodes James, *Eden*, p 430.
11. Shuckburgh, p 327.
12. Avon, *Full Circle*, p 348.
13. Rhodes James, *Eden*, p 432.
14. Avon, *Full Circle*, p 352.
15. Shuckburgh, p 346.
16. Nutting, pp 18, 34.
17. Nutting, p 38.
18. Carlton, p 400.
19. Avon, *Full Circle*, p 424.
20. Rhodes James, *Eden*, p 552.
21. Selwyn Lloyd, *Suez 1956: A Personal Account* (Cape, London: 1978) p 42, hereafter Lloyd.
22. Thorpe, p 493.
23. Avon, *Full Circle*, p 426.
24. Shuckburgh, p 360.
25. Rhodes James, *Eden*, p 454.

26. Rhodes James, *Eden*, p 469.
27. Avon, *Full Circle*, p 428; Rhodes James, *Eden*, p 483.
28. Harold Macmillan, *Riding the Storm 1956–59* (Macmillan, London: 1971) p 105.
29. Rhodes James, *Eden*, pp 471–2.
30. Avon, *Full Circle*, p 437.
31. Dutton, pp 404–5.
32. Avon, *Full Circle*, p 467.
33. Avon, *Full Circle*, p 484.
34. Hennessy, p 231.
35. Rhodes James, *Eden*, p 512; Clark, p 178.
36. Nutting, p 63.
37. Carlton, p 425.
38. Avon, *Full Circle*, p 499.
39. Carlton, p 427.
40. Nutting, p 77.
41. Dutton, p 414.
42. Lloyd, p 160.
43. Avon, *Full Circle*, pp 504–5.
44. Hennessy, p 246.
45. Nutting, p 95.
46. Rhodes James, *Eden*, p 529.
47. Rhodes James, *Eden*, p 533.
48. Thorpe, p 519.
49. Hennessy, p 222; Rhodes James, *Eden*, pp 534–5.
50. Lloyd, p 249.
51. Thorpe, p 563.
52. Dutton, p 427.
53. Edward Heath, *The Course of My Life: The Autobiography of Sir Edward Heath* (Hodder and Stoughton, London: 1998) p 169.
54. Rhodes James, *Eden*, p 549; Clark, p 198; Shuckburgh, p 362.

55. Nutting, p 110.
56. Rhodes James, *Eden*, pp 542–6.
57. Rhodes James, *Eden*, p 558.
58. Thorpe, p 531.
59. Clark, p 209.
60. Avon, *Full Circle*, pp 540, 545.
61. Hennessy, p 244.
62. Keith Kyle, *Suez: Britain's End of Empire in the Middle East* (I B Tauris, London: 2003), pp 405, 432.
63. Lloyd, p 207.
64. Rhodes James, *Eden*, p 565.
65. Howard, pp 236–7; Carlton, p 462.
66. Rhodes James, *Eden*, p 567.
67. Rhodes James, *Eden*, p 576.
68. Lloyd, p 219.
69. Dutton, p 440.
70. Dutton, p 445.
71. Rhodes James, *Eden*, p 586.
72. Colville, p 670.
73. Carlton, p 456.
74. Rhodes James, *Eden*, pp 590–7.

Chapter 8: Conclusion: 1956–77

1. Thorpe, p 606.
2. Thorpe, pp 576, 561.
3. Hennessy, p 208.
4. Thorpe, p 580.
5. Thorpe, p 172.
6. Clark, p 215.
7. Dilwyn Porter, 'Never-Never Land: Britain under the Conservatives 1951–1964', in Nick Tiratsoo, *From Blitz to Blair: A New History of Britain since 1939* (Weidenfeld and Nicolson, London: 1997) p 115.

8. Rhodes James (ed), *Channon*, p 452.
9. Moran, p 530.
10. Thorpe, p 605.
11. Rhodes James (ed), *Channon*, p 382.
12. Clark, p 164.
13. Thorpe, p 226.
14. Dilks (ed), *Cadogan Diaries*, p 345.
15. Dutton, p 184
16. Carlton, pp 339, 109.
17. Nicolson, *Diaries and Letters, 1939–45*, p 344.
18. Clark, p 160.
19. Hennessy, p 207.
20. Shuckburgh, p 73.
21. Dutton, p 466.
22. Nicolson, *Diaries and Letters, 1930–39*, p 252.
23. Harvey (ed), *The War Diaries of Oliver Harvey*, p 144.
24. Moran, p 261.
25. Thorpe, p 263.
26. Rhodes James, *Eden*, p 223.
27. Thorpe, p 262.
28. Harvey (ed), *The War Diaries of Oliver Harvey*, p 162
29. Howard, p 108.
30. Shuckburgh, p 131.

CHRONOLOGY

Year	Premiership
1955	6 April: Anthony Eden becomes Prime Minister, aged 57. May: Conservatives win general election with 49.4 per cent of the vote, increasing their Commons seats from 321 to 345. October: Chancellor R A Butler's budget increases taxes. December: Eden reshuffles Cabinet: Macmillan replaces Butler as Chancellor; Selwyn Lloyd becomes Foreign Secretary.
1956	January: Eden visits USA – warns of Soviet influence in Egypt. February: Macmillan threatens resignation over abolition of milk and bread subsidies: Eden backs down. March: King Hussein of Jordan dismisses General Glubb. July: Last British troops leave Canal Zone under 1954 agreement. USA abandons support of Aswan Dam project. Nasser nationalises the Suez Canal. October: Britain turns to the UN to resolve Suez Crisis. Sévres Protocol: Britain France and Israel agree plan for invasion of Egypt. Israel attacks Egypt at the end of the month. November: French and British land in Egypt; US pressure on sterling forces cease-fire. Eden leaves for Jamaica to convalesce. December: Britain forced to withdraw from Suez by UN.
1957	9 January: Eden resigns, having been in office for only one year and 279 days

History	Culture
Purge of Chinese Communist Party.	Graham Greene, *The Quiet American*.
Occupation regime in West Germany ends.	Vladimir Nabokov, *Lolita*.
USSR annuls its treaties with Britain and France.	Samuel Beckett, *Waiting for Godot*.
Warsaw Treaty establishes Warsaw Pact.	Films: *The Seven Year Itch*. *Rebel Without A Cause*. *The Ladykillers*.
South Africa withdraws from UN General Assembly over Cruz Report on Apartheid.	James Dean dies in a car crash.
	Sony launches first mass-produced transistor radio.
	Commercial television is introduced in Britain.
	TV: *This is Your Life*.
Soviet General Secretary Khrushchev denounces Stalin's policies.	Karl Mannheim, *Essays on the Sociology of Culture*.
Pakistan becomes independent.	First computer-programming language is invented in USA.
USSR abolishes Cominform.	A J Ayer, *The Problem of Knowledge*.
UN obtains agreements of ceasefire between Israel and Jordan, Lebanon and Syria.	Britten, *The Prince of the Pagodas*.
	Lerner/Lowe, *My Fair Lady*.
New government, including non-communists is formed in Hungary. It renounces the Warsaw Treaty. Soviet forces attack Budapest.	Rock'n'Roll dominates the dance floors.
	John Osborne, *Look Back in Anger*.
Fidel Castro lands in Cuba and begins guerrilla warfare to overthrow Batista's government.	Films: *Baby Doll*. *The King and I*. *A Town Like Alice*.

FURTHER READING

Anthony Eden wrote four volumes of memoirs. He began at the end, and ended at the beginning. *Full Circle* (Cassell, London: 1960), covering the post-Second World War years up to Suez, is partial and self-regarding. *Facing the Dictators* (Cassell, London: 1962), covering his political career up to 1938, is slightly less so. *The Reckoning* (Cassell, London: 1965), covering the war years, is by far the best of the political memoirs. *Another World 1897–1918* (Allen Lane, London: 1976), covering his childhood and youth, is the most personally revealing thing he ever published.

D R Thorpe, *Eden* (Pimlico, London: 2003) is the most recent biography. Like Robert Rhodes James, *Anthony Eden* (Weidenfeld and Nicolson, London: 1986), it is mostly sympathetic to its subject. David Carlton, *Anthony Eden: A Biography* (Allen and Unwin, London: 1986) puts the case for the prosecution. David Dutton, *Anthony Eden: A Life and Reputation* (Allen and Unwin, London: 1997) takes a thematic approach and carefully weighs the evidence for and against.

Several of those close to Eden wrote diaries. Two volumes by Oliver Harvey, his private secretary at the Foreign Office until 1943, were edited by his son, John Harvey, and published as *The Diplomatic Diaries of Oliver Harvey 1937–1940* (Collins, London: 1970) and *The War Diaries of Oliver Harvey 1941–1945* (Collins, London: 1978). Those by Alexander Cadogan, Foreign Office permanent secretary, were edited by David Dilks and published as *The Diaries of Alexander Cadogan, O.M., 1938–45* (Cassell, London: 1971). Those by Eden's Foreign Office private secretary in the 1950s were published as Evelyn Shuckburgh, *Descent to Suez: Diaries 1951–56* (Weidenfeld and Nicolson, London: 1986).

Other readable and relevant diaries from the period include Harold Nicolson, *Diaries and Letters, 1930–39* (Collins, London: 1966) and *Diaries and Letters, 1939–45* (Collins, London: 1967); Lord Moran, *Winston Churchill: The Struggle for Survival 1940–1965* (Sphere, London: 1968); and Jock Colville, *The Fringes of Power: Downing Street Diaries 1939–1955* (Phoenix, London: 2005).

The best recent general history of the period is Peter Clarke, *Hope and Glory, Britain 1900–1990* (Allen Lane, London: 1996). Suez has spawned a voluminous literature of its own. Keith Kyle, *Suez: Britain's End of Empire in the Middle East* (I.B. Tauris, London: 2003) is unlikely to be bettered as a vivid general account. Selwyn Lloyd, *Suez 1956: A Personal Account* (Cape, London: 1978) ploddingly explains why he went along with Eden; Anthony Nutting, *No End of a Lesson: The Story of Suez* (Constable, London: 1996) explains more racily why he didn't. On facts, neither account is wholly to be trusted. Jonathan Pearson, *Sir Anthony Eden and the Suez Crisis: Reluctant Gamble* (Palgrave Macmillan, London: 2003) is an interesting recent attempt to put Eden's handling of the crisis in a more sympathetic context.

PICTURE SOURCES

Pages 6–7
Anthony Eden meets Rita Hayworth at a film premiere
in the West End, 21 July 1947. (Courtesy Topham
Picturepoint)

Page 85
Anthony Eden photographed with Winston Churchill
shortly before Churchill's resignation as Prime Minister,
23 March 1955. (Courtesy Topham Picturepoint)

Page 129
Egypt's President Nasser and Eden photographed in the
year before the Suez crisis, 21 February 1955. (Courtesy
Topham Picturepoint)

INDEX

W

THE 20 BRITISH PRIME MINISTERS
OF THE 20TH CENTURY

Salisbury

SALISBURY
Conservative politician, prime minister
1885–6, 1886–92 and 1895–1902, and
the last to hold that office in the House
of Lords.
by Eric Midwinter
Visiting Professor of Education at
Exeter University
ISBN 1-904950-54-X (pb)

Balfour

BALFOUR
Balfour wrote that Britain favoured 'the
establishment in Palestine of a national
home for the Jewish people', the so-
called 'Balfour Declaration'.
by Ewen Green
of Magdalen College Oxford
ISBN 1-904950-55-8 (pb)

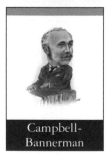
Campbell-
Bannerman

CAMPBELL-BANNERMAN
Liberal Prime Minister, who started the
battle with the Conservative-dominated
House of Lords.
by Lord Hattersley
former Deputy Leader of the Labour
Party and Cabinet member in Wilson
and Callaghan's governments.
ISBN 1-904950-56-6 (pb)

Asquith

Lloyd George

Bonar Law

Baldwin

ASQUITH
His administration laid the foundation of Britain's welfare state, but he was plunged into a major power struggle with the House of Lords.

by Stephen Bates
a senior correspondent for the *Guardian*.
ISBN 1-904950-57-4 (pb)

LLOYD GEORGE
By the end of 1916 there was discontent with Asquith's management of the war, and Lloyd George schemed secretly with the Conservatives in the coalition government to take his place.

by Hugh Purcell
television documentary maker.
ISBN 1-904950-58-2 (pb)

BONAR LAW
In 1922 he was the moving spirit in the stormy meeting of Conservative MPs which ended the coalition, created the 1922 Committee and reinstated him as leader.

by Andrew Taylor
Professor of Politics at the University of Sheffield.
ISBN 1-904950-59-0 (pb)

BALDWIN
Baldwin's terms of office included two major political crises, the General Strike and the Abdication.

by Anne Perkins
a journalist, working mostly for the *Guardian*, as well as a historian of the British labour movement.
ISBN 1-904950-60-4 (pb)

MacDonald

Chamberlain

Churchill

Attlee

MACDONALD

In 1900 he was the first secretary of the newly formed Labour Representation Committee (the original name for the Labour party). Four years later he became the first Labour prime minister.

by Kevin Morgan

who teaches government and politics at Manchester University.

ISBN 1-904950-61-2 (pb)

CHAMBERLAIN

His name will forever be linked to the policy of appeasement and the Munich agreement he reached with Hitler.

by Graham Macklin

manager of the research service at the National Archives.

ISBN 1-904950-62-0 (pb)

CHURCHILL

Perhaps the most determined and inspirational war leader in Britain's history.

by Chris Wrigley

who has written about David Lloyd George, Arthur Henderson and W E Gladstone.

ISBN 1-904950-63-9 (pb)

ATTLEE

His post-war government enacted a broad programme of socialist legislation in spite of conditions of austerity. His legacy: the National Health Service.

by David Howell

Professor of Politics at the University of York and an expert in Labour's history.

ISBN 1-904950-64-7 (pb)

EDEN
His premiership will forever be linked to the
fateful Suez Crisis.
by Peter Wilby
former editor of the *New Statesman*.
ISBN 1-904950-65-5 (pb)

MACMILLAN
He repaired the rift between the USA and
Britain created by Suez and secured for Britain
co-operation on issues of nuclear defence, but
entry into the EEC was vetoed by de Gaulle in
1963.
by Francis Beckett
author of BEVAN, published by Haus in
2004.
ISBN 1-904950-66-3 (pb)

DOUGLAS-HOME
Conservative politician and prime minister
1963-4, with a complex career between the
two Houses of Parliament.
by David Dutton
who teaches History at Liverpool
University.
ISBN 1-904950-67-1 (pb)

WILSON
He held out the promise progress, of 'the
Britain that is going to be forged in the white
heat of this revolution'. The forced devaluation
of the pound in 1967 frustrated the fulfilment
of his promises.
by Paul Routledge
The *Daily Mirror's* chief political
commentator.
ISBN 1-904950-68-X (pb)

Heath

HEATH

A passionate European, he succeeded during his premiership in effecting Britain's entry to the EC.

by Denis MacShane

Minister for Europe in Tony Blair's first government.

ISBN 1-904950-69-8 (pb)

Callaghan

CALLAGHAN

His term in office was dominated by industrial unrest, culminating in the 'Winter of Discontent'.

by Harry Conroy

When James Callaghan was Prime Minister, Conroy was the Labour Party's press officer in Scotland, and he is now editor of the Scottish *Catholic Observer.*

ISBN 1-904950-70-1 (pb)

Thatcher

Major

Blair

THATCHER
Britain's first woman prime minister and the longest serving head of government in the 20th century (1979–90), but also the only one to be removed from office in peacetime by pressure from within her own party.
by Clare Beckett
teaches social policy at Bradford University.
ISBN 1-904950-71-X (pb)

MAJOR
He enjoyed great popularity in his early months as prime minister, as he seemed more caring than his iron predecessor, but by the end of 1992 nothing seemed to go right.
by Robert Taylor
is Research Associate at the LSE's Centre for Economic Performance.
ISBN 1-904950-72-8 (pb)

BLAIR
He is therefore the last prime minister of the 20th century and one of the most controversial ones, being frequently accused of abandoning cabinet government and introducing a presidential style of leadership.
by Mick Temple
is a senior lecturer in Politics and Journalism at Staffordshire University.
ISBN 1-904950-73-6 (pb)

THE 20 BRITISH PRIME MINISTERS OF THE 20TH CENTURY

www.hauspublishing.co.uk

NASSER
by Anne Alexander
ISBN 1-904341-83-7 (pb)

'I am Gamal Abd-al-Nasser. I am for you. My blood is for you....for your freedom and your dignity', shouted Nasser to the crowd, moments after a failed attempt on life, and only days before he was appointed Prime Minister.

Nasser was far from a revolutionary firebrand in 1952, though afterwards he was eager to promulgate the idea that the overthrow of King Farouq was a revolution, rather than a disorderly and drawn-out transition of power. Hardened and ambitious though he was during these years, his vision for Egypt's future was vague. He relied instead on his political finesse and ruthlessness until the Suez Crisis of 1956, which became his great act of political defiance, allowed him to humiliate and defeat the colonial powers he so despised, and transformed him into the champion of the Arab Nationalism.

As Nasser's nationalisation programme strained Egypt's economy in the 1960s, prompting strikes and demonstrations, the Six Day War was already looming on the horizon. His one-day resignation after defeat became inevitable, and the subsequent demand by the Egyptian people that he be immediately reinstated, was a signal of their lasting reverence and adoration for him that even defeat could not tarnish.

A charismatic leader, he came to represent the Arab world's empowerment and assertiveness in a post-imperial age, using paired down rhetoric he addressed his people directly, shunning both the mechanics of government and trappings of power.

With the volatility of the Middle East and the Arab world once again the focus of the world's attention, and with Nasser's most prominent domestic foe, the Muslim Brotherhood, gaining popular support in Egypt, Anne Alexander's timely biography charts Nasser's rise to prominence, and the legacy of Arab nationalism he left behind.